Anxious Attachment Recovery Made Simple

A Pathway to Overcome Relationship Anxiety, Rise Above Clinginess and Overthinking, Cultivate Trust, and Rediscover Independence and Self-Worth

S.C. Rowse & Inner Growth Press

Copyright 2023 -by Inner Growth Press- All rights reserved.

The content contained within this book may not be reproduced, duplicated or transmitted without direct written permission from the author or the publisher.

Under no circumstances will any blame or legal responsibility be held against the publisher, or author, for any damages, reparation, or monetary loss due to the information contained within this book, either directly or indirectly.

Legal Notice:

This book is copyright protected. It is only for personal use. You cannot amend, distribute, sell, use, quote or paraphrase any part, or the content within this book, without the consent of the author or publisher.

Disclaimer Notice:

Please note the information contained within this document is for educational and entertainment purposes only. All effort has been executed to present accurate, up to date, reliable, complete information. No warranties of any kind are declared or implied. Readers acknowledge that the author is not engaged in the rendering of legal, financial, medical or professional advice. The content within this book has been derived from various sources. Please consult a licensed professional before attempting any techniques outlined in this book.

By reading this document, the reader agrees that under no circumstances is the author responsible for any losses, direct or indirect, that are incurred as a result of the use of the information contained within this document, including, but not limited to, errors, omissions, or inaccuracies.

Contents

Introduction 1

1. The Initial Bond 7
   Attachment
   Development of Attachment Styles
   Activity: Creating Secure Attachment
   Key Takeaways

2. Decoding Triggers 27
   Finding Triggers
   Trigger Techniques
   Activities: Keeping a Secure Attachment Journal
   Key Takeaways

3. Managing Anxiety and Regulating Emotions 49
   Strategies
   Practical Techniques for Managing Anxiety

    Strategies For Emotional Regulation

    How to Develop Self-Compassion and Self-Care

    Activity: Self-Care Steps

    Key Takeaways

4. Trauma   67

    What Is Trauma?

    Overcoming Traumatic Experiences

    Activity: Exercises That Can Help You Heal From Trauma

    Key Takeaways

    A Call to Fellow Explorers

5. Rewiring Your Brain for Security   85

    What Is Neuroplasticity?

    Key Takeaways

6. A Journey to Secure Attachment   95

    What Is a Secure Attachment Style?

    Step-By-Step Guide to Secure Attachment

    Question Sheet: Building Secure Attachment

    Key Takeaways

7. Building Trust in Relationships   107

    Building Trust Between the Different Attachment Styles

    Modern Technology and Your Attachment System

    Activity: Trust Evaluation Worksheet

    Key Takeaways

8. Overcoming Self-Sabotage   127
   Stop Self-Sabotaging Behavior
   Activity: Self-Sabotage Awareness
   Key Takeaways

9. Reflection and Next Steps   135
   Continued Growth and Lifelong Learning
   Activity: A Self-Reflection Exercise
   Key Takeaways

Conclusion   140
   Key Takeaways

References links   143

When Feeling Deeply Meets Understanding Deeply   144

Introduction

A thick haze of cigarette smoke flew from my lips as I attempted to write. I'm torn. This story is huge. It's one everyone will read by tomorrow morning, and I'll become known as the journalist who was first on its tracks. However, my judgment was clouded, and so was my cubicle—as if the smoke was some sort of expression of my doubts.

I wish I could write the story with the same clarity I had written all of my others, but uncertainty gnawed at me as I took another look at my obscured notes.

How could I possibly write this objectively? How could I when I knew she was much more than a pin-up girl with platinum blonde hair, red lips, and a birthmark resting on her left cheek? Marilyn wasn't just someone with a breathless voice, a playful persona, and talent. She had all of these things, yes. But through my research, I discovered so much more about you... Norma Jeane.

Known as an icon of beauty and grace, she captivated audiences with her charm. However, behind her glamorous persona and dazzling smile, Marilyn hid something that poisoned her entire world: a thing she barely understood herself.

From a young age, she had a turbulent and unstable childhood. With parents fighting their own issues, she was left emotionally neglected and abandoned. Moving from foster home to foster home, she awaited her mother. It must've been so confusing to a little girl to be without a home.

The early lack of love and care planted seeds of insecurity within her, leading to a deep-rooted fear of rejection and desperation for affection. She yearned for a genuine connection and searched for it in various relationships. I think she simply hoped to fill the void. However, the thing inside her clouded her thinking, and some took advantage of her. Even so, she sought love.

According to my sources, Marilyn was clingy and scared, craving reassurance, validation, and affirmations daily. Her constant need for comfort often pushed her partners away, leading to cycles of heartbreak and disappointment.

The thing inside her made her seek approval and validation from audiences, always striving for perfection and nothing less. She feared criticism and doubted herself. She feared someone would snatch away her success at any given moment. Like she thought this was all merely a dream. Was that why you had taken these pills, Marilyn? Was it to sleep?

So, she had success and was adored by millions. Still, Marilyn felt alone. Behind closed doors, she battled with anxiety and depression. She went to therapy. Not that it did her any good.

Poor girl...

Marilyn's life was cut short, leaving behind a legacy. MONROE: The epitome of beauty and vulnerability. Norma Jeane Mortensen, the little girl seeking a home. Both yearn for love and connection.

I read a study on attachment styles once. I think that's the thing that's been inside Marilyn. Her unresolved feelings, traumas, and attachments. If only I had written about this in the last issue.

I sighed heavily, knowing that this wasn't the story my boss wanted to hear. Not at all. In fact, it wouldn't even make it past my desk. He wanted the gossip, the juicy story of what had transpired earlier tonight.

I'm sorry, Norma Jeane, but today I have to write what they want to hear. So, within a few strikes of the typebars, I spit out my heading:
MARILYN MONROE: DEAD

A Tale of Rest Gone Wrong

Similar to Marilyn Monroe, many of us have fears, insecurities, and unresolved trauma that make it difficult for us to trust others and to feel secure in our relationships. These could also result from childhood trauma, as was Marilyn's case. If you didn't have safe, mentally balanced caretakers available to you as a child, you may still be influenced by your past.

Do you often feel like you're too anxious and possibly over-dependent on your partner in a relationship? Maybe you even struggle to form relationships at all, and you struggle to deal with breakups. The fact is, many of us continue to struggle throughout our lives with a pattern of repeatedly attracting emotionally unavailable partners. We overthink and doubt every move we make in our relationships, and we eventually end up tired of living this exhausting way. Some of us may even experience relationship burnout and think we'll never be able to have a healthy relationship.

If you picked up this book, you're likely struggling with anxious attachment, and we want to help you change your life in a positive way. The more knowledge you have on this subject, the better you'll be able to deal with it.

The book will help you gain a better understanding of anxious attachment while also helping you uncover the root causes and triggers that are causing your relationship struggles. It's always helpful to understand your triggers, as you may not be fully aware of exactly why you're acting in certain ways or responding negatively to certain situations.

By increasing your self-awareness, you can begin a healing journey of personal growth and learn to cope in ways that will help you create and maintain more meaningful relationships.

We understand that you have many reasons for purchasing this book. Maybe one of your friends recommended it after you told them you're struggling in your relationship. Or you've done some self-reflection and realized there are certain areas in your life where you want to grow. We can guide you in the right direction.

You will no longer feel overly dependent on others for reassurance and support. This book will teach you about neuroplasticity, and we will guide you toward forming secure attachments and healthy relationships. When you have a deeper understanding of anxious attachment, you'll have the tools you need to break free from the patterns you've been repeating when attracting emotionally unavailable partners.

We spent years accumulating the knowledge collected in this book, and we can assure you this is the right book for you if you're ready to make a change. You're coming to us for advice, and we're going to give you the best input we can.

We want to provide you with useful, practical advice and guidance to help you navigate your way to long-term change and a better quality of life. With every chapter, you'll be closer to achieving a secure attachment pattern and the rich connection with others that you truly deserve.

We encourage you to take a leap of faith and run this transformation marathon with us until we push you over the finish line. We'll navigate the challenges together and empower you to build strong, loving relationships.

"Anxious Attachment Recovery Made Simple" is a transformative book filled with practical strategies to help you on your journey to healing. For a comprehensive and immersive experience, we strongly recommend purchasing the companion journal. This lined journal is designed to enhance your progress, making your path to recovery even more effective and fulfilling. Embrace the power of both resources to unlock the full potential of your healing journey.

Click here or scan the QR code below to acquire the journal.

We look forward to accompanying you on this path of emotional freedom.

1
The Initial Bond

I lightly tapped my fingers against my laptop keys, pressing hard enough to make a sound but not enough to allow letters to appear in the reply box on Reddit.

I'm always on here. It's a perfect space for advice on mental health and relationships, so that's why. However, it's also an excellent place for people to share their experiences. I don't do this. Well, usually. Today, however, I feel compelled to share.

"Does anyone have any success stories or advice dealing with anxious attachment style," the post read. I'm hesitant, of course, but what if they really need this? What if what I have to share helps them through what they're facing?

While trying to convince myself to respond, I failed to notice how my fingers glided and pushed through the keys, declaring all I wanted to say.

I'm in a relationship, and I adore the man. We've been together for a little over a month, and last week, I sensed him pulling away from me. I kept quiet because I feared coming off as clingy or annoying.

The anxiety started in my stomach, like a pit, and rose to my chest. It was suffocating. Then the thoughts came: "Why is he being distant? Am I driving him away? Is he losing interest? What did I do wrong?" These thoughts, his feelings, and his behavior consumed me entirely.

So, first, I turned to a "protest behavior" of ignoring him. However, this will only cause destruction. I realized that we must communicate our feelings constructively, no matter how hard it may seem.

Thus, I looked toward my sister and called up my best friend to talk about how I was feeling because it helped scratch open the surface to reveal my core emotions. I feared abandonment, which yanked the control I had from my hands.

Once I regained my footing, I texted him and told him what I had observed and how it made me feel. I asked what he was feeling and whether I had done something to upset him. He's a great guy who calmed my nerves and reassured me. I'm Lucky.

With anxious attachment, you need a strategy for dealing with relationship anxiety. First, consider telling them about your attachment style, educating them so that they can understand where you're coming from and gaze into your view of things. Also, never bite your tongue and deal with your thoughts by yourself. They'll eat you up, and it doesn't do anyone good. You don't have to be alone in this. Communication is key. It's hard, I know, but your bond doesn't have to be.

And send...

Attachment

Have you ever wondered how relationships work? Why do we have them? How do they develop? And why do we treat them the way we do? Scientists and researchers wondered the same thing and concluded that the answer lies with the first bond we ever created—the one we shape and hold with our caregivers.

Not so long ago, we didn't know much about our relationships. We simply had them, and when we behaved in certain ways within them, everyone simply stated that it was a part of our personalities or some other thesis.

In fact, some initial thoughts and theories claimed that we only build such close relationships with our caregivers because they were the ones feeding us. Thus, according to this argument, our first relationship was based purely on breast milk, pancakes, and cereals.

Some may look at this theory and say that it adds up, but it left far too many questions unanswered. At the same time, it was the only answer and was, thus, deemed good enough. However, its glory was short-lived when World War II crept near.

In Britain, fathers fought abroad for the *Grand Alliance*, while mothers looked after their children at home. That was until one dreadful day in September when German aircraft bombed London, igniting fires all over the city. Many children were left without homes and caregivers. They had to go to orphanages.

In one of these orphanages, a young British psychiatrist and psychoanalyst, John Bowlby, observed that children weren't thriving even when given proper housing, Medicare care, and food. It simply wasn't good enough.

He noted that the children would cry for their parents, looking at doors awaiting their return. They wanted their attachment figures.

Thus, Bowlby saw the hole within the 'feeding theory' and knew that the tilt of a bottle or scoop of a spoon wasn't the proper answer. Instead, he claimed it all boiled down to behaviors, motivational patterns, and strong attachments.

The Father of Attachment

Bowlby, determined to solve this enigma, turned to nature, noting that humans and animals were very much alike regarding their caregivers and general bonds.

The way these orphans constantly sought after their parents, whether through yelling or waiting, was the same as when a puppy would run to its mother when a stranger tried to catch or harm it. We aren't exactly the same as animals, of course, but we show similar manners.

Bowlby, for example, also noted other similarities in the work of another psychologist, Harry Harlow, who greatly influenced and helped him develop his conclusion, which we'll get to in a minute. First, let's talk about Harlow. He conducted multiple studies and experiments during his career, but his most infamous one focused on maternal deprivation.

In the study, newborn monkeys were separated from their mothers and placed in cages with mothers made of wire. One held a bottle, and the other was covered in soft cloth. Harlow noted that the infants went to the bottle mother for food but spent most of their time with the soft-cloth mother. When frightened, the infants returned to the cloth mother for comfort and security. In sum, it proved that bonds result from comfort and care and not from being fed. Although his work is controversial and cruel, it did prove crucial for Bowlby and his work.

We do need food, yes. However, babies cannot get by on their own. They need someone who takes care of them in all aspects. The orphans, for example, had everything necessary for them to be physically healthy, but there was a key part missing that no one could provide but their caregivers.

Imagine, for a second, you're a baby playing on the front lawn, and out of nowhere, a speeding car hurls your way. Essentially, this means that, yes, you need someone who can feed and shelter you, but in this instance, these two things aren't essential. Papayas can't stop the car, and as morbid as it may sound, a warm bed won't help you survive when tires trek your way. Thus, you need an attachment figure, or caregiver, who can pull you out of your way and toward safety.

As Pediatrician Donald Winnicott, wrote in 1964, "There's no such thing as a baby. If you set out to describe [one], you'll find you're describing a baby and someone else. A baby cannot exist alone..." This is precisely what Bowlby was talking about, a baby needing someone to survive.

In Bowlby's view, everything we do as infants aim to create a close physical bond between baby and caregiver, simply because if this dynamic weren't there, the baby would have a lesser chance of survival. In other words, according to Bowlby, these behaviors weren't random but rather a survival mechanism. It's a so-called evolutionary system we all hold that ensures our species lives on for another day. This is the attachment system.

However, this isn't the whole theory portion; there's still one fundamental aspect. But, before continuing down that road, we thought it was essential to clarify who your 'primary attachment figure' is and what it means to have one exactly.

So, usually, this person is your mother, but it doesn't have to be: it can also be a father, grandparent, aunt, uncle, or someone who took you in while you were young. It's whoever took care of you, primarily, so to speak. Yet, to make this as concise as possible, there are four distinct phases of attachment describing when and how our attachments form. Thus, as outlined by researchers Rudolph Schaffer and Peggy Emerson, here they are:

- Pre-Attachment Stage: Babies do not form attachments to anyone specific between their birth up to three months. We would call this the "signaling" phase because that's what they rely on—signals. They cry, moan, and yell to catch a caregiver's attention. As a result, the caregiver becomes closer to the infant and cares for its needs.

- Indiscriminate Attachment: Infants begin to prefer a particular caregiver over others from a little over a month up to seven months. As they learn to trust one specific person to meet their needs, they'll respond more positively to that caregiver, despite accepting care from others.

- Discriminate Attachment: Between seven and eleven months of age, infants are likely to form strong attachments with a single caregiver and become distressed when separated, often also exhibiting a fear of strangers.

- Multiple Attachments: Anywhere from nine months onwards, children develop strong emotional connections with additional caregivers, such as a second parent, older sibling, aunt, etc.

As you can see, connections are essential, starting from a very young age, and while these stages might seem relatively straightforward, the road to our relationships is far more complex. Not everyone is raised the same, which we'll go into more detail later. However, for now, as promised, let's discuss the next cut of the theory.

Essentially our attachment systems send off alarm bells whenever something "threatening" transpires, whether it's hunger, sleep, love, or something more pressing such as that speeding car. As it chimes, we search for our attachment figures, assessing whether they can meet our needs and provide us with what we want.

Usually, an infant or child needs to be safe, seen, soothed, and secure in that they have a sense of security and trust. Without these things, the ringing bells will continue.

In other words, there were certain attributes present in the bond between caregiver and infant, which Bowlby noted, and compiled together as the "characteristics" of attachment, which were:

- Proximity maintenance: We all want to be near those we feel attached to for comfort, care, and security. Thus, the infant or child will do the same and always seek some sort of 'proximity' with their attachment figure.

- Secure base: Caregivers act as a reliable and sound foundation for the child to walk on, enabling them to explore their surroundings, learn for themselves, and sort through everything confidently.

- Safe haven: While the child is out on their "explorations," they also want to know that they can seek support and return to their attachment figures for comfort and safety whenever scared, threatened, or lonely.

- Separation Distress: The infant or child experiences anxiety or distress when the attachment figure is absent. They want their caregiver, and being away from them seems "wrong" and upsetting.

Although essential, these characteristics aren't enough to truly comprehend the composition and impact attachments have on us.

They're a silicone mold that just sits there—empty. Despite being crucial for creating something, it's not the part we'll use. Thus, what truly matters is what we pour into the mold.

Bowlby noted that it isn't just the connection between infants and caregivers that mattered, but the quality of the caregiver's sensibility and responsiveness to the infant's needs. This makes or breaks the child's emotional growth, social development, and overall well-being.

Thus, if the attachment characteristics weren't met, and the child didn't feel fulfilled or "treasured" by their caregivers, there was a block in the connection, and the infant remembered it. This is the liquid our caregivers have poured into the molds, and we're the end results.

Pattern Recognition

Within the first few years of our lives, and as we grew up, we observed and identified various bits of information from our relationships, especially the one we held with our attachment figure.

Think of our brains as one extensive computer program consisting of video uptake, processing, and data capturing into a spreadsheet. When we observe patterns within our relationships, we upload a video into our minds, write out the information or transcripts, and drag the "impressions" and notes into our mental spreadsheets.

At the end of the day, we use these spreadsheets as they tell us what we can expect from others, how relationships should be, how we should treat them, and what our behaviors should be like. Thus, from a very young age, our mental models begin to take shape, and before we know it, these beliefs turn into traits that we carry through to adulthood.

Yet, this still doesn't answer why your thought process is how it is today. I mean, which videos did you upload? What information did you process? And what types of patterns did you extract into your mind?

What do your spreadsheets say? To best answer this, we must focus on another developmental psychologist and colleague of Bowlby, who built upon his research and created a study known as *The Strange Situation*. Her name was Mary Ainsworth.

The Mother of Styles

When Mary was just 15, she found a passion for psychology after reading a book by American psychologist William McDougall. From there, she obtained multiple degrees, spent several years teaching at the University of Toronto, and joined the Women's Army Corps.

Afterward, she settled down, married, and laid roots in London. During this time, Ainsworth worked alongside Bowlby, researching the bond held between mothers and infants. After leaving this position, however, her work didn't stop.

She spent some time researching in Uganda before returning to the United States, her country of origin and taking up a teacher's position at John Hopkins University.

Here, Ainsworth began constructing an assessment to measure attachments between mothers and infants, and yes, this is where her famous *Strange Situation* study, which we mentioned before, finally found its legs.

Study Objective and Research

Ainsworth's "Strange Situation" experiment sought to identify different attachment patterns between mothers and infants while assessing the children's attachment levels and categorizing them into different attachment styles based on their behaviors and responses. However, at that time, Mary was yet to know about these so-called attachment styles as that part is still to come. For now, however, let's focus on the observational study itself.

In her study, infants and toddlers between 12 and 18 months were placed in a playroom with their mothers. Researchers observed the duo as the child explored and got used to this unfamiliar environment before they started throwing curveballs or "experimental variables" into the mixture.

First, a stranger entered the room and gradually approached the child before the mother was signaled to briefly leave the playroom. After spending some time in the room, alone with the stranger, the mother returned to her child.

According to Ainsworth, although the entire study revealed plenty, how the child behaved once the mother returned ultimately tilted the information regarding the children's attachment ways and told Ainsworth precisely what she wanted to know.

Through these observations, Ainsworth identified three primary attachment styles: secure, anxious-ambivalent, and avoidant. A fourth pattern, disorganized attachment, was added in later research. So, what exactly do Ainsworth's conclusions mean?

To best grasp her concluding remarks, understand the key findings, and what it has to do with us, it's best to go back to the source. Below you'll find a bulletin list, each point starting with one of the attachment styles, followed by some text. The latter is a summary of the reactions and behaviors we're after.

- Secure: initially, these children showed a balance between seeking proximity and feeling secure enough to explore the unfamiliar room freely. They were also friendly towards the stranger. When the mothers left, however, the children explored less, were wary of the stranger, and showed signs of distress. Upon her return, the children reacted positively, were easily comforted, and bounced back quickly. They simply went on about their explorations like nothing had happened.

- Avoidant: these children either didn't explore the room much or only focused on doing this and nothing else. They treated the stranger like they did their mothers, showing little concern for the fact that they were there. After the mothers left, the children weren't really phased by their absence or being alone with a stranger. With her return, they also didn't seek proximity or comfort; instead, they avoided eye contact and tried their best to ignore her, which is probably why some focused on exploring—to avoid their caregivers altogether.

- Anxious-Ambivalent: they didn't explore much on their own and were wary of the stranger. They became highly distressed, anxious, and insecure when their mothers left. When she returned, their behaviors weren't one and the same: they wanted to regain that closeness with their mothers, clinging to them. Even so, they showed resentment and anger toward her for leaving. Her attempts to comfort them were likely resisted and did little to settle or soothe them. It was clear that they were never truly secure.

- Disorganized: although this attachment style was only identified later, they could be described as children showing a mix of styles, mainly appearing confused, disrupted, and uneased. For example, when the mothers returned, they wanted to approach her for comfort but were scared to do so as well, leading them to take on an "approach and retreat" manner, where they showed odd behaviors such as freezing or fidgeting and moving in ways that didn't really make sense.

As you can see from the list, each attachment style showcased a variety of emotional and behavioral reactions once their relationship was thrown into the story.

It's important to note that multiple things can shape and set how you form and handle your connections, whether it's something you experienced as a child or an adult. It doesn't have to be because of your caregiver.

However, we find the Strange Situation procedure especially noteworthy as it was done on infants and toddlers alone. It showed that the attachment with your caregivers could be the weight tilting the scale of your attachment style. The initial bond is, thus, your very first determinator.

We know, we know, we've made this point throughout. Nonetheless, it's important because it's the first pattern you put into your mental spreadsheets. Most often, these are the imprints you carry around, whether you're 13 or 20, even when you don't realize it.

Don't get us wrong; we're not saying there's something wrong with not being raised how you wished to be raised or because your caregivers strayed away from the "ideal" household. "It's life," as they say, and various events and things happen to us all. You don't have to feel ashamed or aggrieved. We mention all of this purely for your own benefit.

Take Ainsworth's findings, for example; she gave us a peek into how we might've used our patterns and spreadsheets as children and, possibly, how we still use them as adults today.

As adults, however, things get more tricky, and the stakes are raised. Remember, most of what we do is about emotions, thoughts, beliefs, and relationships.

Want to own successful e-commerce? It's a desire and thought you have. You either believe in yourself enough to think you can achieve this, or you don't. It's about your relationship with yourself, and along the steps of the ladder, you'll have to make more connections to ensure that a strong network has your back. You can apply this straightforward formula to almost every aspect of your life.

Yet, you also have to remember that these aspects mentioned above, and every part of your life, can be influenced by your attachment style. This means that you can blur how you view yourself, treat others, and perceive the world around you while managing your emotions and handling any hardships can become tedious tasks to do. All your relationships are on the line, whether with a friend, partner, or yourself. Thus, it's all about affinities.

Look, we all experience different versions of relationships as we grow older. For example, the relationship you shared with your caregiver isn't the same one you'd share with your partner.

However, underneath the nature, roles, and all, the foundation of your relationships are all the same. Your initial bond is the start of your Jenga tower. From there, you just add pieces, whether placed neatly or askew. No matter what you do, you still have that first layer of blocks holding everything together: the foundation of your thinking, beliefs, relationships, and ways. You keep building the height, but it's still the same tower.

Psychologist Theodore Waters once stated, "There's a thread connecting life in your mother's arms and life in your lover's arms," this is precisely what we, Bowlby and Ainsworth, were getting at.

There's a casual transfer of our ways, emotions, and beliefs like they were merely left stuck to our little socks. Now, even though our shoe sizes have grown, we wear the same old socks.

You, for example, might've grown to become uneasy and alert toward threats in your relationships. The worries, whether you know it or not, often grasp control. You've likely had this attachment style throughout your life, or maybe you don't know. What you do know is that you treat your relationships the same as when you did when you were just a baby, longing for a caregiver who made you feel the way you wanted to feel.

Development of Attachment Styles

They say there's nothing stronger than the bond of a family and that no one can ever break the relationship between a parent and their child. This important relationship also influences the development of different attachment styles, which will continue to affect the child's life into adulthood. Let's take a more in-depth look at how the various attachment styles are developed.

The type of attachment style you've developed would depend on the caregiving you would have received during your early childhood years. You would have developed a secure attachment style if your caregiver was responsive and sensitive. This doesn't simply mean that you were showered with hugs and kisses but also that your caregiver really listened to you and acted in a way that made you realize you mean a lot to them. This behavior would also have been consistent, and you would have known what to expect from them. This means your caregivers would also have been good at regulating their moods; they wouldn't have been loving at the one moment while lashing out and screaming at you as soon as they got stressed. Caregivers might not always have been able to stop themselves from behaving in inconsistent ways, e.g., if they suffered from mental health issues or addictions. However, even then, it would have helped you a great deal if you had at least one consistent caretaker in your life. Even children who had to deal with abuse or other forms of childhood trauma usually fare better in adulthood if they had at least one person on their side, and it didn't necessarily have to be their primary caretaker.

Children who received responsive caretaking would develop positive views of themselves and others.

Individuals who have developed anxious attachment styles may have received inconsistent caregiving. Maybe your caretakers were there for you at times, but they couldn't always give you what you needed. When they were unavailable or treated you in dismissive ways, you would have felt anxious, and you became clingy and looked for constant attention from anyone who noticed you. Unfortunately, your neediness probably made the people you needed most back then even more impatient with you. You've carried this trait into adulthood, and this causes your romantic partner, and even your friends, to become impatient with you.

If you have an avoidant attachment style, you may like to think of yourself as very independent and think that you need no one else in your life. You don't like anyone getting too close to you, even your romantic partner, and you need your alone time. If you have a partner with an anxious attachment style, this could cause problems in your relationship, as you could become drained and annoyed by their constant need for reassurance and attention.

If you have this attachment style, your caregivers were likely distant or neglectful. Maybe their lives were simply too stressful to give you all the attention you needed, for example, if they were a single parent, they could have been working several jobs just to put food on the table. If you have a whole bunch of siblings, they possibly just didn't have the time to give you all the attention you needed.

They could also have been uncomfortable with emotional expression, and from the example you've set, you've learned to express your emotions into adulthood. Ultimately, avoidantly attached children will distance themselves emotionally and prioritize independence over seeking comfort.

You could have developed a disorganized attachment style when you loved your caretaker, and they loved you, but you also regarded them as a source of fear. For example, they give you love and attention but scream and lash out at you as they struggle to control their mood swings, which is very confusing and scary, leaving you unsure of how to react during stressful times. Some people also develop this attachment style as a result of trauma.

In the next chapter, we consider how trauma can trigger you and how you can deal with these triggers.

Activity: Creating Secure Attachment

The following exercise can help you develop a secure attachment style:

- Find a quiet space where you won't be disturbed. Find a comfortable position, sitting or lying down.

- Imagine yourself in your favorite safe place. This could be anywhere from a beautiful garden to the beach or your childhood bedroom.

- Use all your senses while you're imagining yourself in this environment. Notice the sounds, colors, textures, and scents around you. Experience the warmth of the sun on your skin, and listen to the soothing sounds of nature around you.

- Imagine a supportive person coming into your favorite safe space. This could be someone from your past who has made you feel safe and secure. You could also create a new person who embodies love and emotional support.

- As this person approaches you, imagine their comforting

presence. Allow yourself to feel safety and acceptance in their presence. Feel their warm embrace and hear their soothing words.

- Take note of how you feel. Do you feel valued and understood?

- Stay in this visualization for as long as you feel peaceful and secure.

- When you're ready, bring your focus back to the present. Take some deep breaths, and slowly open your eyes.

- Write about your experience in your journal, and take note of any insights you may have gained. Consider how you can bring elements of your visualization into your daily life to develop a more secure attachment style.

- Do this exercise as often as you want. It could assist you develop a more secure attachment style over time by helping you feel safe and more emotionally resilient.

- If you feel you need additional support, reaching out to a mental health professional who specializes in attachment issues may be helpful.

Key Takeaways

- Our relationships in later life are influenced by our first relationships with our childhood caretakers.

- Children are very dependent on the adults with whom they

form relationships during the first years of their lives.

- The baby's primary attachment figure would be the person who mainly cared for them when they were young. This doesn't necessarily have to be their mother.

- There are four distinct phases of attachment.

- During the pre-attachment stages, babies don't form attachments to a specific person between their birth to three months.

- When infants are in the indiscriminate attachment stage, they start to prefer a certain caregiver above others.

- In the discriminate attachment stage, babies are between seven and eleven months and form strong attachments with a single caregiver. They will become distressed when they're separated from the caregiver and show a fear of strangers.

- The multiple attachment stage develops from nine months onwards. They form emotional connections with many different caregivers.

- If the attachment characteristics weren't met, and the child didn't feel fulfilled by their caregivers, they would remember this in adulthood.

- Our childhood relationships give us a template of what we can expect from our adult relationships.

- The three primary attachment styles are: secure, anxious-ambivalent, and avoidant.

- The disorganized attachment style was introduced later.

2

Decoding Triggers

―――ele―――

Hi, I'm Sarah, and I'm a "recovering anxious attachment type."

I know it sounds like the start of an awful sitcom, but there wasn't anything funny about it at the time. So, somewhere in my early 20s, I realized that I not only needed but deserved someone available and didn't jump into the relationship with that "hit-or-miss" mindset. Been there, done that, and I was fed up. However, to fix my past strays, I "overcorrected," and by a long shot... I married someone who I wasn't all that crazy about.

He was stable, secure, and I felt safe with him. On paper, he checked all the right boxes. So, I thought the whole thing about love having to "sweep you off your feet" was simply some glamorized myth created by playwrights and directors. As you can imagine, I'm divorced now.

After some time, I got back onto the dating horse and relapsed. All of those awful anxious attachment thoughts came rushing back. I couldn't understand it. I knew I was a good catch! Still, if those words didn't come from someone else, the doubts would just burst through the front door and stay on the couch for days.

I got nervous, like really nervous. It also didn't help that the first person I connected with after my marriage had ghosted me. I know, who does that?! I thought it only happened on TV, but no, it happened, and my ego took a brutal hit!

Nonetheless, I persevered and kept looking in the mirror daily, saying, "You're a good catch!" and "If they don't match your energy, they're not for you, Rah!" Self-proclaimed nickname aside, I won't lie and say that I still don't deal with these occasional thoughts, even though things have gotten better, way better.

I'm dating someone, and he's completely different than anyone I've ever dated. He was your stereotypical "bad boy" with a deviant past. In fact, he's still got that rockstar charisma and flirtatious way about him. He's also sensitive, open, honest, vulnerable, and aware of himself and his struggles.

He tells me exactly how he feels about me, which usually would've sent me running for the hills, if I'm honest. I've always feared intimacy and growing close to others. Stepping out when someone got needy was much easier. I had to look out for numero uno, no matter who I hurt. That was until he came along.

Our connection didn't scare me at all! I've given in to him entirely because of how safe, secure, comfortable, and worthy he's made me feel. I could be myself around him; he just "got" me and gave me what I needed in a relationship. Ironically, he stated I was the only reason he felt comfortable enough to soften up and let down his guard in the first place.

I hit the jackpot, ladies and gentlemen, as he's just a wonderfully rare species who's an excellent example for my son and makes me a fantastic model for my daughter. In sum, we bring out the best in each other.

I've realized you can never settle because you're scared of the "what ifs" because what if you miss out on the person who was made for you? And, oh boy! When you find that person, as I have, those subtle anxious triggers come up but fall quicker because you're finally sure.

So, yes, perhaps this does sound like some awful start to a rom-com or sitcom, but I wouldn't have it any other way.

Finding Triggers

Sometimes, it seems like life is going well. We have everything under control, our relationships are doing good, we're happy, and our anxious "symptoms" seem to be fading... but then it happens. While walking in the sun, you suddenly take one wrong step and hear a metallic clicking sound. You look down, only to find a landmine.

You have two choices: either stand your ground and wait for help or move your leg and allow it to explode. We often choose to move.

However, when we make this choice, these hidden landmines within us burst, and like some emotional tripwire, they send feelings, memories, traumas, and thoughts rushing through our minds. Then, we simply can't help but believe we're back at square one.

These landmines, or triggers as they're more commonly known, often lurk under various situations and stimuli within our lives, coming forth in multiple shapes and sizes, customized to fit each individual's unique history and experiences. It's warfare and most definitely personal.

However, just like how landmines are difficult to understand due to their complex nature, hidden presence, and potential danger, so are triggers. Your spurs could differ from ours, and you might still need to learn what yours are. We know, "Where do I start? How do I know?" and all the other questions. Recognizing and identifying everything can be tough when you do it alone. Fortunately, you've got us.

Together, we'll explore some of the more common spurs that lie in wait when you have an anxious attachment style, and then we'll help you identify the ones you hold. So, that's what we'll do here today.

The Triggers for an Anxious Attachment Style

If you have an anxious attachment style, you have a heightened need for closeness, and you could fear being abandoned by your partner or loved ones.

If you have an underlying anxious attachment style, it's likely that the following situations might trigger you:

When a partner is emotionally unavailable and doesn't provide validation or support, it could cause you to feel anxious, and you may feel like they're about to leave you. You may even feel frustrated when your partners just express anger or frustration or when their contract with you decreases for a while. This could also cause you to fear rejection.

You could also be triggered if you feel you're being forgotten or ignored. This could cause conflict in relationships as you might expect people to react immediately to your text or social media messages, and you could feel that you're being deliberately excluded from social events, even if this isn't the case. You may also feel overlooked and neglected in group settings when the attention isn't on you.

You could be struggling with disagreements and conflict, as you fear that it will end at the end of your relationship.

Criticism or negative feedback could also be triggering for you. You might see it as a personal attack on you, even if the intention was just to give you feedback on how you could improve.

People will have different triggers, and not everyone with an anxious attachment style will experience the same ones. If you can become more self-aware, you'll have a better understanding of your specific triggers.

Personal Landmines

Even when faced with the triggers above, you might still need to learn which triggers are yours. Thus, we wanted to ensure you know exactly what you're working with by giving you a small "Landmine Detecting Kit" you can use to ensure you know exactly where all of your triggers lie.

Before that; however, we wanted to read the label or slogan slapped onto the back; an additional tool, if you will, or even the main thing that will help you finally get the best of your triggers, and it's all about keeping your "why" in mind.

So, if a deminer went out searching for landmines and, halfway through, forgot what he was doing, he would likely die, right? Now, even though you wouldn't 'perish' per se when you fail to remember why you want to be more securely attached and aware, you risk forgetting to acknowledge triggers, implement tools, and work toward your goal. You could even forget everything you'll learn in these books.

In short, as the label reads: "Failure to remember the "why" might result in the explosion of all mines." So, with that said, let's unzip the kit and go through all the tools to identify your triggers:
1. Reflect on your past experiences, relationships, and interactions with others. While doing so, look for patterns that consistently trigger your anxiety or insecurity. Consider spe-

cific events, behaviors, or circumstances, as these are often important cues that help you find your triggers.

2. Focus on feeling and healing your traumas. Once you push through this process will allow you to regain sensitivity, start healing, and take the necessary steps toward minimizing your triggers and becoming securely attached.

3. Observe and monitor almost everything: your thoughts, beliefs, emotions, and even your body, for any possible signs of triggers. Paying attention to everything is essential. Let's observe this:

   a. Emotions: Notice what elicits strong emotional responses such as fear, jealousy, or insecurities from you. These emotional reactions are often indicators of your triggers. So, if you're feeling anxious, overwhelmed, or inconsolable and don't know why, you might be triggered by some situation or perceived behavior.

   b. Thoughts and beliefs: It's important to be mindful of your thoughts and beliefs about yourself, others, and your relationships. Triggers can often stem from negative perceptions or deep-rooted fears. So, if you notice any recurring negative thoughts or moments of self-doubt, try and pull them apart and find the core reason as to why that is.

   c. Physical sensations: If you experience any physical discomforts, such as tension in your muscles, shallow breathing, or an increased heart rate during specific interactions or situations, don't ignore them. These sensations can provide valuable clues to your triggers. So, once again, find the core reason.

4. Do you seek constant reassurance or validation from your employer? Become overly worried or anxious when your friends don't respond promptly or spend time with others? Are you often wondering whether or not your partner still wants you in their life? These are all patterns worth noticing because they can help you identify triggers and why they exist in the first place. So, when someone spends time with someone else, for example, this would be your trigger stemming from a fear of being abandoned or not being good enough.

5. Be open and willing to listen to yourself and to what your whole being is saying. Never brush something off as insignificant because you think so or because we haven't mentioned it. We're all unique, and your triggers might not look like the next person's. You have to go into this journey with intent. So, intend to be receptive and hear the messages your body is sending, whether apparent or static.

6. Whenever you pick up on any signals, ensure you stop to breathe, take a moment to yourself, reflect, and think about what is causing you to feel triggered. Never allow anything to go unchecked or unresolved. Identify everything so that you can later deal with everything.

Anything that results in solid emotions or pattern-like behaviors should be noted. You must do some work and discover as much as possible about yourself, your history, and why you're feeling and acting the way you are. It won't be an easy ride, of course.

It's perfectly normal to struggle with the identification process, as it's an ongoing process requiring self-reflection, self-awareness, and loads of patience. It's challenging work for the anxious attachment type because, let's face it, you've been through a lot, physically, mentally, and emotionally. At times, you'll struggle to be sensitive enough to take on your past and traumas, which is fine. However, these triggers and core problems cloud your attunement and keep you from being securely attached. We want this for you. Therefore, even though it might be uncomfortable, it's needed and most definitely worth it.

By finding and understanding your triggers, you can develop healthier coping mechanisms and finally work towards building more secure, clear, and fulfilling relationships with those around you and with yourself.

To help you along, keep a self-reflection journal or turn to a supportive friend, partner, or family member. These approaches can make it easier to foster self-awareness and uncover the patterns your attachment mines might reveal while ensuring you never miss a step. So, just try different methods until you find what works for you.

Also, know that you don't have to do this alone. You could, for example, consider professional support from a therapist or counselor specializing in attachment theory and relationships. We all need that lending hand from time to time, and there's nothing wrong with seeking help in identifying and exploring your triggers. However, if you don't want this, that's fine, too. As long as you find some triggers, we're all good.

So, that's the toolkit—unwrapped and ready to help you find your spurs. With that said, it's about time we move on and tackle some strategies to help you manage your triggers and reduce their impact on your life. So, are you ready?

Trigger Techniques

If you wish to handle triggers and reduce the casualties they have in your life, you must self-regulate. But what is it anyway?

Essentially, it's a process all about your thoughts, feelings, beliefs, and behaviors. It involves looking inward and examining everything to ensure you achieve some goal or outcome. For us, this would be confronting and dealing with your triggers.

Simply put, self-regulation is the tool that allows you to know and understand everything there is to know about yourself and your internal states.

If you look at the previous section, for example, you'll find that you were practicing self-regulation to some degree while finding your triggers: same thing, different goal.

In our eyes, the whole ordeal is absolutely essential if you want to manage emotional reactions and behaviors in a healthy and balanced manner.

So, when you're anxiously attached, your emotional responses are more intense, and your behaviors are often maladaptive. It's because you have these unresolved wounds and fears in the center that leads your way.

With self-regulation at your side, however, you can override your usual ways and channel them into positive patterns that help you deal with your triggers calmly and constructively. You'll also find emotional stability, healthy relationships, positive thoughts, clear communication, and independence regardless of what others think or do. Yes, all of this is possible with self-regulation. Now, all we need are some more specific tips.

Anger Management

We all get angry, regardless of attachment style. How we deal with emotion, however, is another story.

Unfortunately, when you're anxiously attached, your underlying fears, insecurities, past experiences, and attachment wounds might make you "angrier" than most, significantly affecting you and your relationships.

Think of the anger like a tall brick wall, built and enclosed in a circle, with some barbed wire across the top. It keeps the bad things out, offering protection and defense. However, it makes it hard for whatever's inside to come out. We suppose you could say it's a blessing and a curse.

We get it, though. Sometimes it's easier to express anger than to deal with more intense, raw thoughts, feelings, and problems. Sometimes, it might be that you're unable to express yourself otherwise, either not being ready to face the core problem or finding it "easier" to do than saying what's actually bothering you or what you need, or want to say.

Not everyone with an anxious attachment style will exhibit more anger as our emotional responses may vary, and our rage might manifest differently. However, these general recommendations are aimed at helping you with any anger you have, whether hidden or not, as well as any you might come across in the future. So, just remember this as we run through the tips to help you keep the red-flamed emotion in check.

Lowering the Heat

Amid a heated argument, it feels like you can barely control your emotions and words. You get so caught up in your anger that all logical thinking and considerations go out the window, leaving only regrets and scars you can't take back. That's why you should never talk things out while you're mad. Instead, remove yourself from the situation and take a few minutes to yourself. Focus only on calming down by:

- Going for a walk or jog.

- Talking to someone about your feelings.

- Practicing relaxation techniques. Meditate or take a few good, deep breaths.

- Finding humor without being rude or inconsiderate.

  - For example, Psychologist Dr. Jerry Deffenbacher suggested you draw the silliest version of how you view yourself in arguments, such as a supreme leader who can do nothing wrong. Make the drawing as extravagant and outlandish as you can. Doing this will stifle a laugh and push you into a better head space.

There are so many things you can do. So, if something's healthy and constructive while also good at calming you down and getting you into the right mindset to think clearly—do it!

Once you've regained your composure, you're going to have to put on your thinking cap. Consider what made you feel this way, especially any underlying causes such as fear or rejection, and how you'll express it to the other person. Remember to stay calm while reflecting, as you don't want sparks flying onto the steel wool.

Then, turn to their perspective and try to understand where they're coming from. What's bothering them? Do they have any underlying fears or problems? How can you handle it or make them feel better?

Think of the problem, solution, and conclusion from both ends.

Then, when everything is clear, and you're ready to talk things out and so are they, sit down in a comfortable, safe space and focus only on effectively communicating without reheating the pot by:

- Slowing down and carefully thinking about your responses.

- Expressing frustrations, concerns, and needs without being confrontational or demanding. Explain where your anger stems from.

- Use "I" statements where possible, such as "I feel upset when you...."

- Make solutions open so that the person doesn't feel like you're trying to control them but that you're merely suggesting ways to end the conflict.

- Listen attentively to what the other person is saying. Consider their thoughts, feelings, and any underlying struggles they may have.

  - Don't interrupt the other person, dismiss their feelings, play the blame game, or gear up a screaming match.

  - We know it's natural to want to get defensive when criticized, but do your best not to fight back.

Last, but not least, remember that anger gets you nowhere, and if you hold onto it, it will eat you up. Thus, never hold a grudge and try your best to pardon others. Forgive and forget; that's key, as with it comes peace, which you most definitely deserve.

Now, we can only imagine you've just read that, shook your head, and scuffed, "Easier said than done!" We know, we know. However, to do this, you must give yourself time, space, love, and respect.

Remind yourself that you must let go of things, if not for them, for yourself. Only then will you be able to move and truly be happy.

More on Anger

Furthermore, as you'll note, many of the tips mentioned above can be used in other situations where you're anger simply gets the better of you. So, these tips aren't just limited to arguments.

Exercise, for example, is a great way to shed stress, which gravely contributes to our anger. Thus, whether or not you're coming down from an argument, tie your exercise sneakers and get physical.

However, before we go on and on, it's best to lay down another bulletin list showcasing ways to manage your anger when someone isn't yelling back:

- Take small breaks where you work through your thoughts, relax, and prep for the rest of the day.

- Distance yourself from the "source" of your anger.

- If your partner left the bathroom a mess, close the door.

- If a friend isn't responding, leave your phone alone and do something else.

- Note angry patterns and "consider the clock."

- For example, if you're not a morning person and constantly get into arguments around that time, change when you talk about serious stuff so that conversations don't spiral into arguments.

- If your anger has gotten out of control or you can't handle it alone, don't be afraid to seek professional help.

Furthermore, remember to forgive and forget those who frustrate and anger you, as stated previously, and use the same humor approach for other situations, such as drawing yourself as some "Gordon Ramsay" chef throwing the cold pizza the delivery guy brought you, and then forgive him, too.

Mindfulness

Have you ever been completely absorbed and focused on your surroundings, actions, and emotions? This is precisely what being mindful is all about—being fully present in the moment and aware of who you are, where you are, what you're doing, how you're feeling, and more. Sounds simple, right? Still, as you probably know, it rarely is.

Unfortunately, struggling to remain mindful can be even more complicated when you have an anxious attachment style. When you're anxiously attached, you tend to overthink, fear losing control, react emotionally, worry, and obsess while seeking constant reassurance and validation from others. Your fears, traumas, and other attachment "symptoms" are intense and can get a lot.

All of this can, understandably, make it hard for you to stay in the present and engage in mindful practices simply because your attention is consumed and preoccupied. You're essentially programmed to always prepare for the "what-ifs" while spewing thoughts and beliefs that hinder your ability to stay mindful of your experiences and self. Ironically, you stand to gain the most from this practice, especially when dealing with triggers.

Triggers usually follow a set pattern of experience and then reaction. With mindfulness, however, you create another piece in the equation: A pause, which allows you to think and react more thoughtfully and rationally.

You'll also learn to view triggers as passing events and not things you should define yourself because you're so much more. You'll discover how to live in the moment without judgment and distraction while reducing stress, building resilience, improving mental health, and enhancing your overall quality of life.

Lastly, you'll finally learn how to slow down, appreciate the finer things, and cultivate a sense of inner peace and clarity that puts those pesky triggers in their place.

In short, you stand so much to gain. Here are a few tips to help you become more emotionally intelligent and mindful in your daily life:

- Set a clear intention to be more mindful. Understand why you want this, how it can benefit you, and what you wish to achieve.

- Incorporate yoga practices such as Asana, Pranayama, or Meditation into your routine. You can start doing this once a week for a few minutes before gradually increasing the duration.

- Pay attention to your experiences, sensations, and emotions throughout the day. Engage in all you do, whether walking, eating, or talking to someone.

- Observe your thoughts, feelings, experiences, and sensations without any bias or attachment. Notice them as they come and go, but don't put labels like "good" or "bad" on everything.

- Give yourself time and space to digest experiences and feelings. Intentionally create that "pause" between your triggers and reactions.

- Be compassionate toward yourself, recognizing that feeling emotions and negative thinking is okay. We all have bad days. Just accept, feel, and let go.

- Take "mindfulness" breaks where you reset your mind, disconnect screens, remove distractions, and focus on improving mindfulness only.

- Explore other mindfulness resources, such as books, courses, or apps that help deepen your understanding and perspectives. Various mindfulness practices, techniques, and exercises exist, so simply find one that resonates with you.

My final advice is to practice kindness, patience, and compassion toward yourself while practicing mindfulness. Remember that this requires time and effort. As they say, "Rome wasn't built in a day," and one of these days, you'll find a finely built domus decorated in marble and travertine, where you'll finally be present.

Grounding

Nothing quite prepares you when triggers boil over into reality. Your thoughts and emotions often take over your entire body and mind, making it hard to "take a breath" and "think before you act" simply because it gets too much. This is where Grounding steps in.

Aimed to shake you back to the present, it helps you regain your footing and brings stability and security back into your life while calming your mind, body, and soul. To do this, we wanted to discuss a few grounding techniques that can help you when the going gets tough:

- Deep breathing: take slow, deep breaths with one hand on your abdomen. Breath in through your nose and exhale through your mouth. Focus on your hand bobbing up and down as you breathe. Focus on each exhalation and inhalation that passes through your body.

- Engage senses: focus on your immediate surroundings, noticing what you can see, hear, touch, taste, and smell. Anchor yourself to the present by admiring the sun's warmth or the sweet smell of the neighbor's freshly cut grass.

- Grounding objects: carry things you can touch or hold when triggered, such as a stone or trinket. Note whether it's smooth, bumpy, cracked, heavy, or cold to the touch. Evaluate until your focus is back.

- Self-soothe: engage in activities promoting relaxation and self-care, such as taking a warm bath, stretching, or engaging in hobbies you enjoy.

- Self-Affirmations: repeat positive affirmations to yourself, such as "I'm safe," "I'm present," or "I can handle this," to remind yourself to remain calm, positive, and sure of yourself.

Remember, however, that your experience with some grounding techniques may vary and that finding what works best for you is essential. All the tips and techniques mentioned are merely a foundation for managing anxiety, promoting a sense of security, living in the present, and finally, showing your triggers who's the boss. Thus, make it work for you.

Cognitive Change

Our minds often get scattered by negative thoughts and unconstructive beliefs. It's human. However, when this way of thinking changes our way of living, it isn't good. To fix this, we must pull together the pieces of our minds and rearrange the ideas and perspectives we hold into more favorable patterns. In short, we must reconstruct our cognitive ways.

Cognitive reconstructing is aimed to challenge and transform our distorted ways of thinking and leaves our minds more balanced, realistic, and constructive. Essentially, it's like we're cleaning out a home and replacing all the run-down furniture with some new units. You're like this interior decorator slash cleaner of your mind, painting over negative thoughts and limiting patterns to leave behind a better color scheme. You give everything a good clean, which means more secure, positive, and fulfilling relationships with yourself and others. Plus, your worries are reduced.

In short, it all starts and ends with your mind, and because this is where cognitive restructuring darts its attention, you can only stand to benefit and grow from this. So, the only question that remains is how we can truly change your mind, hold the patterns, and allow you to thrive. We'll take a look at this in the next chapter.

Activities: Keeping a Secure Attachment Journal

The aim of keeping this journal is to help you develop a more secure attachment pattern through self-reflection and personal growth.

Set aside time for this activity and find a quiet space where you can do some introspection. You can keep your journal in a physical book or on one of your electronic devices. Write in your journal as regularly as possible as a form of self-reflection and self-care.

Once you're ready, consider the following:

- Think about past situations or relationships that could have contributed to your anxious attachment style. Consider how these experiences have influenced your emotions, behaviors, and thoughts. Have you identified any triggers, patterns, or themes?

- Explore your attachment-related needs and fears in your journal, and make a list in your journal. You can use this for validation, intimacy, fears of rejection, or abandonment. Take the time to consider these needs and fears and acknowledge how they have been significant in your relationships.

- Recognize negative self-talk and self-limiting beliefs you may have about attachment, and write them down. Question their validity, and attempt to replace them with more compassionate and realistic affirmations.

- Write a letter in which you offer yourself as support and guidance. Acknowledge your progress, and show yourself empathy and understanding as you work towards developing a secure attachment.

- Make a list of qualities that are associated with secure attachment, such as trust, healthy boundaries, or self-care. Think about how you can embody and incorporate these qualities in relationships.

- Think about the triggers you've identified in previous exercises. Consider and write about each trigger in detail. Unpack the emotions, thoughts, and sensations the triggers evoke. Think about alternative ways in which you can respond to the trigger. What actions or coping strategies can help you navigate them?

- Write down at least five positive things in your life that you're grateful for, as well as positive affirmations to emphasize your growth and resilience.

Key Takeaways

- Emotional triggers are events or stimuli that could cause a strong emotional reaction. These can be based on past experiences or personal experiences.

- Triggers can cause intense feelings like fear, sadness, or anger.

- Pay attention to your emotions to discover what your triggers are. What elicits responses like fear, jealousy, or insecurities from you?

- Consider if your triggers could result from negative perceptions you have of yourself.

- When you notice that you're having negative thoughts or experiencing self-doubt, try to find the core reason why this is happening.

- If you experience unpleasant physical sensations such as muscle tension, fast heartbeats, and shallow breathing, pay attention to them, as they can give you clues about your triggers.

- We're all unique, and your triggers might not be the same as someone else's.

- Developing healthier coping mechanisms can be achieved by recognizing and understanding your triggers.

- Self-regulation is the ability to regulate your emotions, thoughts, and behaviors. To do this, you need to be aware of your internal states and how they affect your behavior.

- If you have an anxious attachment style, you might struggle with excessive anger, potentially affecting your relationships.

- If you can't handle your anger, you should consider looking for professional help.

- Learn to see your triggers as passing events and that they don't have to define you.

- Grounding connects you with the present moment and makes you feel stable and calm. Attention is directed away from distressing thoughts, emotions, and memories and focused on the immediate physical moment.

3
Managing Anxiety and Regulating Emotions

Progress Notes:
Dr. Ardal Balliol / Tranquil Haven Therapy / Client Name: Emily Maya

Date: 25/06/2021 / Session Start Time: 4 P.M. Session / End Time: 4:55 P.M.

In today's session, the patient experienced a significant breakthrough. She expressed a newfound understanding regarding her anxious attachment patterns and the healing process. She realized that healing did not entail eradicating all feelings of anxiety but instead acknowledging and allowing herself to feel her emotions without letting them define her self-worth. She felt a sense of pride in her progress and the insights she had gained.

The patient mentioned having an experience with her former romantic partner earlier this week, where he reached out to her because he was leaving the country shortly. She admitted that the interaction triggered a sense of anxiety. We explored the emotions surrounding the event and how it was linked to her attachment history.

We worked on validating her feelings and fears while fostering self-compassion and recognizing her growth in managing such situations more constructively. She acknowledged that the intensity of the anxiety was no longer as overwhelming and approached these feelings with curiosity, trying to understand them, allowing them to pass before moving on. She displayed significant growth in not letting this anxiety dictate her life or impact her self-esteem.

Furthermore, the patient found solace in realizing that the interaction with her former partner didn't harm her personal growth or well-being. Instead, it served as a poignant reminder of how far she had come on her healing journey.

The patient also expressed a keen interest in sharing her experiences and lessons with others struggling with anxious attachment, such as teaching them how to cope through various strategies and tips. She demonstrated a profound understanding of the importance of living consciously and accepting feelings regardless of intensity or fluctuations.

Overall, the session was marked by the patient's growing awareness and willingness to embrace her emotional journey with resilience and self-understanding.

At the end of the session, I acknowledged her progress and emphasized the importance of her celebrating this breakthrough and the progress she had made over the year.

After reviewing recent developments and updating her on her current status, I assured her of the continued support she has in navigating relationships that may challenge her familiar patterns.

I encouraged the patient to continue nurturing her self-awareness, self-esteem, and attachment concerns using the strategies we've developed in previous sessions. I asked her to write one or two pages of a book aimed at helping others deal with their anxious attachment style. By engaging in this process, I hope she can solidify her understanding of the insights and strategies while fulfilling her desire to share her experiences with others if she wishes to publish the book someday.

Looking ahead to the next session, we'll explore the content she wrote for the book and discuss any reflections or emotions that arose during the process. This strategy should become an enriching and empowering experience for her.

I also plan to revisit the topic of her former male companion as she prepares to say her final goodbye. I anticipate this moment might trigger feelings related to past traumas and experiences of abandonment. While I have confidence in her ability to work through these emotions, we must ensure she can manage and regulate her emotions effectively.

Session Scheduled - Monday, 4 P.M.

Strategies

We've all experienced people who struggle to deal with daily life. Maybe you've worked with a boss who got upset at the smallest mistakes as if it was the end of the world. You could have been raised by parents who were perfectionists and couldn't deal with it when life threw curve balls at them, which upset their ideas of perfection. This wouldn't have set a great example to you, a young child at the time, and might even be why you struggle to deal with your own emotions as an adult.

Struggling with managing our emotions is a common human experience, and it's nothing you need to be ashamed of. You can learn skills and strategies to become better at this.

Remember that it's vital to manage your emotions as they will also determine how you behave toward others and how you react to the information you receive from them. This will also determine how healthy your children are overall. Interaction with others is so much easier if you can keep a tight grip on your emotions and communicate in an objective way, even when you're upset about something.

Your emotional management strategies can be anything from breathing techniques to a healthy lifestyle. If you feel like you need expert guidance, don't hesitate to make an appointment with a therapist.

Also, look for support from the people around you, whether from your family and friends or by joining support groups. Support groups are useful, as you can learn a great deal from the experiences of others.

What Is Emotional Dysregulation?

Do you often feel overwhelmed and angry when small things go wrong in your life? Do you lash out at others when the pressure becomes too much? You might be struggling with emotional dysregulation.

This means your emotions could be intense and unpredictable, and it's a battle for you to control them and respond to them in healthy ways.

Your struggles could result from neglect or abuse you experienced in childhood, especially if your caregivers also struggled with emotional dysregulation and couldn't model healthy coping behavior.

It's normal to feel anxious during stressful times in your life and experience symptoms such as a fast heartbeat or sweaty palms, but it becomes a problem when it interferes with your daily life.

Unfortunately, emotional dysregulation can make your anxiety worse. For example, when you're angry or upset about something, you might be worried that you cannot calm down.

The interaction between emotional dysregulation and anxiety can create a self-perpetuating cycle where one constantly influences the other and makes you feel worse overall.

Practical techniques, such as breathing techniques and progressive muscle relaxation, can help you manage your emotions and anxiety levels.

Practical Techniques for Managing Anxiety

You can use breathwork or special breathing techniques to feel calmer and more in control of your life. These techniques can help you feel more relaxed and take control of your emotions.

Breathwork exercises will also help you increase your self-awareness as they allow you to become aware of your thoughts, emotions, and sensations in your body.

Breathwork can also improve your physical health by boosting your immune system. You will take in more oxygen and improve your lung capacity and ability to regulate your core temperature.

Your ability to deal with physical pain will improve. Pain makes our bodies tense, and deep breathing can release some of the tension. So where do you start? It may all seem confusing at first. However, we will provide you with some useful information about breathing techniques that will point you in the right direction.

Useful Breathing Techniques

The following are some helpful breathing techniques that could help you manage anxiety.

Diaphragmatic Breathing

Diaphragmatic breathing is also known as deep belly breathing or abdominal breathing. This means you use your diaphragm muscle intentionally to breathe deeply.

This technique emphasizes breathing into the lower belly rather than shallow chest breathing. The aim is to inhale deeply through the nose and allow your abdomen to expand fully. This type of breathing can help you relax and reduces stress.

You can practice it by sitting or lying down with one hand on your stomach. Your other hand should be on the side of your chest. Breathe in, and notice how your stomach expands. When you exhale, your stomach will become flatter.

Holotropic Breathing

The aim of this type of breathing is to bring you into an altered state of heightened consciousness through practicing repetitive movements and breathing patterns. This altered state can also make it easier for you to deal with past trauma.

During holotropic breathing sessions, you should lie down and breathe in a fast, rhythmic way. Don't pause between the time when you inhale and when you exhale.

Pranayama

Pranayama is actually a group of breathing exercises. The name comes from the Sanskrit words prana, which means "life force," and ayam, which means "to extend." When you do these exercises, you aim to control and expand your life force energy, or prana, through breath control and regulation.

It consists of different techniques, each with its own benefits. For example, when you practice alternate nostril breathing, Nadi Shodhana, you should inhale and exhale through one nostril at a time. Kapalabhati involves forceful exhalations through the nose, which will energize your body and clear your mind.

The most practiced pranayama technique is the *ocean-sounding breath*, which can improve your focus and calm your mind. Take a moment to sit or lie down and take a few normal breaths. Exhale slowly and completely.

Rebirthing

Rebirthing is a process of metaphorical "rebirth." Rebirthing focuses on continuous and conscious breathing. By practicing this method, you can release emotional and physical tension, promote self-awareness, and encourage personal growth. Rebirthing sessions typically involve lying down and engaging in deep, connected breaths without pausing between inhalation and exhalation.

These sessions are usually guided by a trained instructor or breathwork practitioner who provides a safe environment.

Progressive Muscle Relaxation (PMR)

Progressive muscle relaxation (PMR) helps your body relax and will make it easier to manage your emotions.

PMR is particularly good for muscle relaxation, as you tense and relax the different muscle groups in your body.

Relaxing your body via the PMR method will reduce your stress levels. When you tense and release your muscles, you'll release the physical tension caused by stressing your body. When your body is relaxed, it will also send signals to your brain that will help you improve your overall well-being.

When you practice PMR, you'll become more aware of the sensations you're experiencing in your body, which will also help you identify stress and manage your emotions better.

PMR will get you so relaxed that it stops you from overthinking and will also stop your negative thoughts in their tracks. You'll just feel so much more in control in challenging situations.

Strategies For Emotional Regulation

It's important that we're able to manage our emotions in a healthy way. We'll all get along so much better, and we can prevent unnecessary fights and misunderstandings. Journaling is helpful, as it can help you understand your emotional triggers and where they originated.

Distractions such as hobbies are helpful, as they can take your attention away from your intense emotions, at least for a while, and help you figure out how to manage your emotions best.

Therapies such as Emotion-Focus Therapy (EFT) can also be helpful.

Journaling

Journaling involves writing down your thoughts and feelings to better understand yourself. It's a great way of practicing self-reflection and gaining more insight into your psyche.

It provides you with a private space where you can express your emotions and deal with them. You're completely safe, and you don't have to worry about what others think about you.

Writing in your journal regularly can help you deal with stress and anxiety and boost your mental health by helping you manage your emotions.

It's a healthy way to deal with those overwhelming emotions that you might not want to share with others. Maybe you don't want others to know what you're thinking, but you still want to get toxic emotions such as anger and sadness out of your system. Journaling can help you prioritize the challenges in your life, track your emotional triggers and develop healthier ways to cope with them, as well as develop more positive self-talk by dealing with your negative inner voice.

Journaling can also help you with problem-solving, allowing you to analyze challenging situations and explore different perspectives. You can gain new insights and find alternative solutions to problems as you write. It can also give you a more objective view of your emotions as you gain distance from them.

There is no correct or incorrect way to keep a journal. You need to find a way that works for you, whether it is by using prompts or writing in a free-flowing way. You can write in a notebook on paper or keep a journal on one of your electronic devices. The best way to keep journaling going in the long term is to do it in a way that fits in with your lifestyle.

When you're writing, let your ideas flow, and don't worry too much about spelling and other mistakes. The most important thing is to get your thoughts and emotions down on paper. If you're not much of a writer, you could even draw your thoughts.

Distraction Techniques

Distractions may not directly resolve the underlying issues causing the emotions. Still, they can provide temporary relief and give you a mental break which will help you gain a new perspective on events.

Distraction is something you would do, even if it's only temporarily, to take your attention away from difficult emotions. If you ruminate about difficult situations and emotions, it can make you feel more out of control. While you're distracted, the emotion will decrease in intensity and will become easier to manage.

Once the feeling is less intense, you can then try to manage it in another way, for example, by going running, painting, or whatever other activities you enjoy doing. Healthy distractions can help you become more resilient and improve your ability to deal with difficult emotions in the long run.

Emotion-Focus Therapy Techniques (EFT)

Emotionally Focused Therapy (EFT) is a type of therapy that is useful when it comes to understanding and dealing with your emotions. This therapy recognizes that attachment patterns and the way we connect with others influence our emotional well-being and how we manage our relationships.

It's a way of talking to a therapist who can help you understand why you feel the way you do and how it affects your relationships. The therapist creates a safe and supportive environment where you can talk about your experiences and how you feel about them. Some of us rather prefer talking to a stranger about our emotions, especially if we feel they might be too much for the people close to us. A therapist is safe to talk to about your emotions, as they won't hold anything against you.

EFT can help you create secure attachments in your personal relationships. It's based on the idea that partners should create a secure and safe environment for each other, enabling them to develop good self-esteem and manage their emotions.

How to Develop Self-Compassion and Self-Care

Many of us have a tendency to be hard on ourselves, and we force ourselves to keep going and get the work done, even if we're not physically or emotionally in a good space. Often it's because we've been raised with a certain work ethic, which tells us that we're only important when we get the job done and please others. We may find it difficult to believe that we even deserve self-care, and often we think we need to deserve it first.

However, being kind to ourselves and practicing self-care can help us manage our anxiety and regulate our emotions.

To have compassion for yourself, you must first acknowledge that you're suffering and going through a difficult time. It's about deciding how you can comfort and care for yourself when you experience challenges in your life.

Judging and criticizing yourself during times of failure or struggle can do more harm than good. After all, no one is perfect, and failure is a part of life. It's a vital part of personal growth—we have to learn from our failures, grow and move on.

The Elements of Self-Compassion

Self-compassion consists of three interconnected elements. These elements can help you develop a nurturing and supportive mindset towards yourself.

Self-Kindness

Self-kindness is about treating yourself with understanding and gentleness, even during challenging times. It's about not treating yourself in a self-critical or judgmental way but treating yourself with compassion and empathy. You would respond to your pain or mistakes with the same kindness you would offer to your family members or friends. When you're faced with setbacks, self-kindness allows you to comfort and support yourself and can also boost your resilience.

Common Humanity

Common humanity is about realizing that suffering, mistakes, and imperfections are part of the human experience. You need to understand that everyone has difficulties and failures in their lives. Most people face emotional struggles at some point. Embracing this common humanity can help you see that your struggles aren't unique. This sense of connection can also promote self-compassion and increase your self-acceptance.

Mindfulness

As discussed previously, mindfulness is about being present in the moment without judgment. It's your ability to observe and acknowledge your thoughts and feelings without getting carried away. Mindfulness allows you to develop a balanced and compassionate awareness of yourself, which allows you to respond to your challenges with clarity and calmness.

What It's Not

There is a tendency to label self-compassion as many different things.

The following can't be regarded as self-compassion:
- It's not about pitying yourself or developing a victim mentality. It's not about exaggerating your suffering but acknowledging it with empathy and supporting yourself.

- It's not about being self-indulgent, avoiding responsibilities, and giving in to all your desires. It's about making decisions that will promote your long-term wellness and happiness rather than looking for instant gratification.

- While self-compassion and self-esteem are related, they are not the same thing. Self-esteem is often based on judgments of self-worth and can fluctuate based on external achievements or comparisons with others. Self-compassion is about self-acceptance and self-kindness, even if you haven't achieved everything you set out to do.

- Self-compassion is not about being selfish or ignoring and disregarding the needs of others. It can help you create more empathetic relationships with others.

- It's not a form of self-criticism. If you're self-compassionate, you can recognize and accept your shortcomings and mistakes without harshly judging yourself. You can respond to yourself with kindness and understanding.

What Is Self-Care?

Self-care should be an important aspect of our daily lives, and we shouldn't first have to deserve it by working until we get sick. Self-care is about caring for your physical, mental, and emotional well-being. It helps you deal with stress and ultimately experience a better quality of life.

Self-care is more complex than it might seem at first glance. It shouldn't be about buying yourself sweet treats after you've worked hours into the night and you've met a pressing work deadline. Instead, it's about caring for yourself in a way that ensures all your emotional and physical needs are met. You need to pay attention to self-care in all aspects of your life. For example, it won't be effective to eat nutritious food every day if you drink too much alcohol and you never get a good night's sleep.

The different forms of self-care can include the following:

- Physical self-care: this can mean exercising regularly, getting enough sleep, eating nutritious food, practicing good hygiene, and attending medical check-ups.

- Emotional self-care: recognize and express your emotions, take part in activities you enjoy, receive support from friends and loved ones, practice mindfulness and relaxation techniques, and engage in hobbies or creative outlets.

- Mental self-care: doing activities that stimulate your mind, such as reading, solving puzzles, learning new skills, practicing meditation or deep breathing exercises, but also getting therapy or professional help if you should need it.

- Social self-care: working at establishing and maintaining healthy relationships, enjoying spending time with loved ones and friends, setting boundaries in your relationships, and seeking social support when you need it.

- Spiritual self-care: this means you take part in activities that foster a sense of connection to something greater than yourself, such as meditation, prayer, spending time in nature, or you take part in religious ceremonies.

If you've suffered from trauma at any point in your life, prioritizing self-care is crucial. We will consider how you can overcome trauma in the next chapter.

Activity: Self-Care Steps

You can pamper yourself while also celebrating your achievements.
You need the following materials:

- Bathrobe

- Bath salts or bubble bath

- Scented candles

- A playlist of your favorite music

- Treat of your choice, e.g., chocolate, fruit, a favorite snack

1. First, set a relaxing and soothing mood. Dim the lights, light your scented candles, and play your favorite music.

2. Prepare a relaxing bath with your favorite bath salts and bubble bath. As the bath fills, picture yourself letting go of your stress.

3. Enjoy the warmth and comfort as you sink into your bath. Take deep breaths, close your eyes, and let go of the worries in your mind. Focus on the warm water enveloping your body and enjoy the soothing scent of bath products.

4. Treat yourself to your snack as you're soaking in the bath. It could be anything you enjoy, from chocolate to a healthy alternative, such as a piece of fruit. Mindfully eat your snack by enjoying its texture and flavor.

5. Once you've finished your snack, take the time to express your gratitude and the positive experiences you've had in your life so far. Also, think about how far you've come and the personal growth you've experienced. If you feel like doing this, write down a list of things you feel grateful for in your journal or on a piece of paper. This could be difficult to do while you're in the bath. It might be easier to do if you have a little whiteboard and markers. You could even have two whiteboards that you put up somewhere in your house; one for gratitude and another one for affirmations.

6. Relaxing in the bath by yourself is the perfect opportunity to work on positive self-talk and think about positive affirmations. Positive affirmation could be something like "I am proud of myself for managing to get my degree while working full time."

7. When you're ready to get out of the bath, wrap yourself in your bathrobe or soft towel. If you have the time, take part in extra self-care activities, such as applying cream to your body, stretching, and doing some light exercise, or just sit comfortably and enjoy the peace and quiet of the moment.

Key Takeaways

- If you feel overwhelmed by your emotions and everyday things that go wrong in your life, you may be struggling with emotional dysregulation.

- If you suffer from emotional dysregulation, your emotions could be intense and unpredictable.

- Emotional dysregulation could also cause mood swings and make it difficult for you to cope with stress.

- Emotional dysregulation and anxiety can be linked to the anxious attachment style.

- You could have developed an anxious attachment style due to your relationship with your childhood caregivers. This might mean that you fear abandonment and rejection in your relationships.

- Practical breathing techniques and progressive muscle relaxation can help you manage anxiety.

- When practicing Progressive Muscle Relaxation (PMR) will help your body relax by tensing and relaxing and tensing the different muscle groups in your body.

- PMR can distract you from negative thinking by focusing your attention on the physical sensations of your body.

- Emotion-Focused Therapy Techniques (EFT) will help you

understand how to deal with your emotions with the help of a therapist.

- Distractions can help you deal with uncomfortable emotions by providing temporary relief and a mental break.

4

Trauma

―✐―

I had just gotten back from the hospital, and to say that I was tired would be an understatement. Throwing my jacket over the chair, I kicked off my shoes and sat down on the edge of my small single-sized bed.

I'm staying at my mom's house until I can figure things out. Everything's just spiraled out of control, and I have no idea how to get everything back in place. With a sigh, my head falls to my hands, my fingertips gently tugging through my matted strands.

As I was about to lie down, in the corner of my eye, I saw a box. It was filled to the top with marble-printed notebooks, neatly placed on top of one another, the dust carefully wiped away.

"I thought you'd like to have them here,"

I looked up at my mom, who stood in the doorway, holding a bowl of steaming Ramen Noodles. She entered and placed the bowl on the desk by the door before turning around to walk out. "Maybe they can help again." She stated, gently smiling before she left.

I didn't know what to think or feel. I had almost forgotten about them. Yet, even after all these years, merely seeing them made it feel as though my insides were still connected to the writing they held, like a single string dangling from an outworn t-shirt.

The bed creaked as I stretched to pick up the box, lifting it up to rest on my lap. 'Book 1: We're Much Alike." The cover read. I smiled gently, but it wasn't a normal smile, like the one you'd give to a stranger on the street; it was because I'd remembered you, Dad.

As I flipped open the first page, it told stories of a sad man who locked himself away in a tower, surrounded by a fire-breathing disease that made him very angry, distant, and cold toward his family. 'It wasn't his fault,' the notes read; he was just sick. However, the princess, his daughter, didn't always know that.

For the first few years of her life, the King's cruel distance slashed wounds inside of her, you see, and it continued to scare and chip away at her as she got older. With mood swings, reckless behaviors, and a mind that never seemed quiet, she leaped from kingdom to kingdom, and prince to prince, never finding the correct potion or spell to fix the gaping itch in her chest and head.

She also wrote of the somber day the bellman yelled, "Hear ye, hear ye, the King is deceased."

He had given up, renounced his throne, and left the princess all alone without answers, reasons, or affection to show.

Then there was the day the princess learned of her incurable disease, the same ick her father had. She knew she would suffer the same fate as him but didn't give up. She searched far and wide for answers and cures. However, amid her journeys, she found something else.

She realized she was much like the king and that he couldn't help himself. The disease made her who she is and him the man he was. It wasn't his fault; he was sick...

That was the last entry I had made of you.

I thought I was "cured" of my so-called 'Daddy issues.' I mean, I moved on; I got married. Sure, it was the wrong call, but still, I tried. I tried so desperately. But here I am, after trying to end it all, just as fate predicted.

Tears trod down my cheeks, burning as they fell onto the pages. As I shifted to readjust my position, A photo of you with Mom and I fell from the pages.

I traced your outline carefully.

You died because you couldn't heal and learn to live with the emotions you feel. For that, I'm genuinely sorry. I know you didn't wish to cause me harm. You didn't know any better, after all. But I'm hurt by you, your actions, and lack thereof. I can't walk the same plank as you did, Dad. I can't.

Wiping my face with the back of my sleeve, I pulled out my phone from my pocket, opening my notepad. As the keyboard sprung onto the screen, I started to type: "My Second Chance."

What Is Trauma?

Trauma is a difficult or scary experience that can leave a strong and even lasting impact on us. We could develop traumas after we experience something dangerous, frightening, and upsetting, and it can determine how we feel and act. Trauma can be physically and emotionally dangerous to people.

We can experience trauma after accidents, natural disasters, bullying, abuse, or after the loss of loved ones. It has been shown that childhood trauma can leave a lasting impact on children if they don't receive support, which can affect them in their adult lives. Childhood abuse can leave deep emotional scars and make it difficult for people to trust others, and feel safe, even in their adult lives. Childhood neglect can also be regarded as a form of trauma.

How Traumatic Experiences Can Contribute to an Anxious Attachment Style

Alice grew up in a home where her parents were often absent. Although she got everything she needed and had clothes, food, and more toys than she could ever play with, she didn't receive attention and love.

Her parents were often busy with work and entertainment, and their neglect made her feel alone. Her parents weren't very nurturing and also tended to be critical. They sometimes made nasty comments about her appearance, and they were never happy with her school marks, even though her teachers were satisfied.

Alice became anxious and worried and grew up believing that her parents didn't value and love her. She developed an anxious attachment style and constantly looked for reassurance and validation from the other people in her life. This caused problems in her relationships, as her romantic partners and friends all saw her as needy and clingy. Her romantic relationships usually didn't last long.

If, like Alice, you suffered from emotional or physical neglect or any form of trauma during childhood, you could have developed an anxious attachment style. You may have developed anxiety and insecurity at this time of your life that followed you into adulthood.

Emotional or verbal abuse could have made you afraid of starting relationships as an adult. Will your adult partners, like your childhood caregivers, find that you aren't good enough and reject you?

You may have an overwhelming fear of social criticism and rejection if you come from a home where you were always not enough or neglected as a child.

Physical abuse could cause intense fear or anxiety, which could lead to an anxious attachment style. People who have suffered through this may always be on guard and avoid situations or people who could trigger memories of their past negative experiences.

Ultimately, trauma can have a strong negative impact on a child's trust in others. They could become scared of forming close relationships, as they always expect to be hurt or rejected.

Overcoming Traumatic Experiences

There are various therapies and practices that can help you deal with trauma. Besides mindfulness and the practical techniques discussed in this book, therapy is always a valid option.

Let's look at some of the techniques that can help you overcome trauma.

Cognitive Behavioral Therapy (CBT)

If you went through traumatic experiences at any time in your life, these may have caused you to develop negative thought patterns ad beliefs. CBT can help you replace the irrational fear that you may have developed with a more realistic response. This type of therapy helps you restructure your thoughts and change your emotional responses and behavior. For example, if you had an accident while doing something, you might be scared to do it again. However, CBT can help you overcome your fear and carry on.

Let's take a more in-depth look at CBT and how it works. We'll focus on Alice again.

Alice felt anxious and worried about going to parties or social gatherings. She was always scared people wouldn't like her or that she would embarrass herself. This negative thinking made her feel nervous and tense, and she started avoiding social events altogether.

Alice decided to seek help and started CBT with a therapist. During their first session, the therapist asked Alice to talk about her feelings and what went through her mind when she thought about social events. Alice said she had negative thoughts like that she wasn't interesting enough or that others would judge her.

The therapist helped Alice in evaluating the evidence supporting and contradicting her negative thoughts. He asked her to think of times when she had enjoyable social interactions or received positive feedback from friends. This helped Alice realize that her negative thoughts weren't entirely accurate. She had felt comfortable in certain social situations in the past. She realized that she was especially good at having one-to-one conversations with people.

The therapist encouraged Alice to challenge her negative thoughts and that she should stop avoiding social events. He suggested that Alice should expose herself gradually to more social situations. She started with small gatherings and gradually attended bigger ones, which helped build her confidence, and made her realize she had better social skills than she had initially thought.

The therapist also gave Alice homework. She had to practice her positive thinking and behavior in real-life situations. Alice attended a dinner party with some of her friends, where she replaced her negative thoughts with more positive ones. She noticed that she felt much less anxious, and she enjoyed the company of her friends.

After several CBT sessions and practice of exposing herself to social situations, Alice's negative thoughts started to lose their grip on her. She realized she had the power to change how she thought and felt.

Imaginal Exposure

Imaginal Exposure is part of CBT that helps people process their traumatic experiences in a safe and controlled way. It can help you a great deal, especially if you struggle with PTSD or other anxiety-related conditions.

The purpose of this treatment is to gradually expose you to the memories of the traumatic event or distressing experience. Instead of avoiding unpleasant memories, you're encouraged to tackle them in a safe setting with the help of a therapist.

Let's take a more in-depth look at Imaginal Exposure by considering Sarah's example.

Sarah had been having nightmares every night about a traumatic experience. She felt anxious and on edge, and she decided she needed the help of a qualified therapist.

During their first session, Sarah shared her distressing memories with the therapist and described how the incident made her feel vulnerable, scared, and constantly on guard.

The therapists guided Sarah through various Imaginal Exposure exercises. He created a safe and supportive environment and made sure that she understood he would support her all the way.

First, she had to describe the traumatic event to the therapist, as well as the emotions she experienced. The therapist made her repeat the exercise over several sessions. She began to feel more in control of her emotions as the traumatic memory became less intense.

As time went on, she tried other techniques with the guidance of her therapist. Sarah learned how to challenge negative thoughts related to the event, which also helped her develop healthier coping strategies.

As the months passed, she had fewer nightmares. Sarah also felt more at ease in her daily life. She knew that the memory of the traumatic event would always be part of her life, but she now had the skills to manage it.

Other Therapies

There are several other therapies that can also help you deal with trauma.

Eye Movement Desensitization and Reprocessing (EMDR)

EMDR is a type of therapy that had been designed to help people deal with traumatic memories and reduce their intensity. Guided eye moments or other types of bilateral stimulation are used while you think about traumatic events. For example, someone with PTSD might use this therapy to work through their distressing memories to help them cope with their daily lives.

Support Groups

If you've experienced trauma, you might benefit from therapy in a group with others who have suffered from similar trauma. If you feel the need to do this, you can share your story with others and learn from their coping strategies. You can provide each other with the empathy and validation you need.

Art and Expressive Therapies

Art can also help you express your feelings, especially if you don't want to talk about them and you feel you're not much of a writer.

You don't have to be a great artist or even good. It's just about getting your feelings out there in any creative way that appeals to you, whether drawing, painting or by doing a collage. Many people find it simply much less threatening to express their emotions through drawing and painting.

Body-Oriented Therapies

These therapies focus on the connection between trauma and its impact on the body. It can help you release the tension that's been stored up in your body and deal with any chronic pain you've been experiencing as a result of abuse.

Experiential and Psychodrama Therapy

Experiential and psychodrama therapy uses role-playing and creative expression to explore emotions, memories, and interpersonal dynamics.

In Experiential Therapy, you'll also participate in activities like art, music, or movement to express your feelings. The therapist will help you process and discuss the emotions and memories in your artwork. This can make it easier to deal with your feelings and help you heal.

As a part of Psychodrama Therapy, you'll act out a situation from your past or present, such as a difficult conversation you've had with a family member or friend, to help you better understand how you can handle situations like this in the future.

Outdoor Adventure Therapy

Do you enjoy moving your body and being outside? Outdoor therapy could be especially useful to you, especially if you struggle with addiction. This type of therapy takes place in nature and uses outdoor activities to promote healing, personal growth, and self-discovery.

Just imagine; you could go on hikes with beautiful views, fishing trips, rock climbing, kayaking, or camping. These activities can help you become more resilient by overcoming your personal challenges. The challenges are structured according to the client's real-life obstacles to form part of the challenges.

Outdoor Adventure Therapy also emphasizes teamwork and communication. When you're part of a group, you have to rely on and support each other. This therapy can also help you if you have trust issues and you're social skills aren't what they should be.

Acceptance and Commitment Therapy (ACT)

Acceptance and Commitment Therapy (ACT) helps people cope with life changes and emotional challenges. The main idea behind ACT is to accept our thoughts and feelings without trying to push them away or control them. It will help you embrace your emotions and make your choices based on what matters to you.

In ACT, we recognize that everyone experiences painful emotions and struggles in life. Rather than trying to eliminate these feelings, we learn to be kind to ourselves and that feeling sad or anxious is just part of being human.

Mindfulness is also a key concept of ACT. Since it's about paying attention to the present moment, it can help us to become more aware of our thoughts and feelings, which will help us respond to them more thoughtfully.

For example, you might be going through a difficult time at work or in your personal life. You're starting to feel overwhelmed, and you try to push your negative emotions away. In ACT, you learned to practice mindfulness and acknowledge your emotions without judging them.

ACT can also help you identify the most important things to you in your life. These values could be things like having a family, taking care of your health, or having a successful career. When you know your values, you can make choices and actions that align with your values.

For example, your health and well-being are important to you. You have multiple work deadlines, and you feel stressed. However, despite being busy, you take regular breaks throughout your workday to go for walks and to eat healthy food. You continue to make choices that support your value of good health, even though you experience challenges.

Acceptance and Commitment Therapy (ACT) teaches us to accept our emotions, and by identifying our core values, we can make choices that lead us toward a more meaningful life.

Trauma Healing and Altering Attachment Patterns

We all have healing potential within ourselves. It can be extremely challenging to deal with and heal from trauma, but overcoming it and embarking on healing and growth is possible with the right support.

We've shown you that mindfulness practices, therapy, and supportive group work are available to help you deal with your traumatic experiences.

Overcoming trauma is the first step toward changing our attachment patterns. When we heal our past wounds, we can start to transform the ways in which we interact with ourselves and others. By challenging our negative beliefs, we're able to develop healthier coping strategies, and we become more resilient when it comes to dealing with life's challenges.

Healing from trauma will also help you to feel safer, build trust with others, and become more emotionally available. These are essential components of secure attachment.

In the next chapter, we consider how neuroplasticity can help your brain recover and help you overcome trauma.

Activity: Exercises That Can Help You Heal From Trauma

There are several useful exercises that can help you deal with your trauma.

CBT: Challenging Your Thoughts

Trauma often leads to negative and distressing thoughts. You can challenge these thoughts to promote a more balanced way of thinking.

When you experience distressing thoughts, ask yourself the following:

- What evidence do you have for these thoughts, if any?

- Can the situation be viewed in different, more realistic ways?

- What would I say to a friend who's had similar thoughts?

Grounding Techniques

Grounding techniques can help you focus and bring you back to the present moment. It can help you manage your emotions when you feel anxious or stressed.

You can do a grounding exercise by following these steps:

1. Start by finding a quiet and comfortable place to sit or stand.

You can do this exercise anywhere, whether you're indoors or outdoors.

2. Take a few slow, deep breaths. Breathe through your nose, hold your breath in for a few seconds, and then exhale slowly through your mouth. This helps calm your body and mind.

3. Look around and identify five things you can see in your environment. Pay attention to their colors, shapes, and textures.

4. Focus on four things you can touch with your hands. It could be the texture of a chair, the softness of a blanket, or the smoothness of a wall.

5. Listen carefully and recognize three different sounds you can hear. It might be the sound of birds chirping, traffic outside, or clock ticking.

6. Take a deep breath and notice two different smells around you. It could be the scent of flowers, food, or even the smell of fresh air.

7. If possible, notice one taste in your mouth. You can take a sip of water or chew on a piece of gum to help with this step.

Journal Writing Exercise

Writing about your thoughts, feelings, and experiences can help you express your feelings.

Expressing your emotions honestly can help you deal with trauma and find a way to move forward.

Key Takeaways

- Trauma is a difficult or scary experience that leaves a lasting impact on someone. Trauma could also be physically and emotionally dangerous to people.

- Childhood trauma can leave a lasting impact that follows children into adulthood.

- Childhood neglect can also be a form of trauma.

- Someone who experienced emotional or verbal abuse might fear establishing relationships in the future. Children who experienced childhood abuse may be scared of rejection or criticism when they establish relationships in the future.

- There are different techniques that can help you overcome trauma, such as Cognitive Behavioral Therapy (CBT).

- Eye Movement Desensitization and Reprocessing Therapy (EDMR) involves guided eye movements and other types of bilateral stimulation.

- Support groups may be useful for those who have experienced trauma, as you can learn from the experiences of others.

- Art and expressive therapies are useful for people who find it difficult to express themselves in words.

- Body-oriented therapies focus on the connection between trauma and its impact on the body.

- Experiential therapy explores emotions and memories by using creative expression.

- In Psychodrama therapy, people act out situations from their past or present with the help of a therapist.

- Outdoor therapy takes place in nature and uses outdoor activities to use healing and personal growth.

- When it comes to Acceptance and Commitment Therapy (ACT), the aim is for us to accept our thoughts and feelings without trying to push them away or control them.

- Overcoming trauma is the first step toward changing attachment patterns.

A Call to Fellow Explorers

A good, sympathetic review is always a wonderful surprise.

thank you

In the heart of your journey through the captivating landscapes of "Anxious Attachment Recovery Made Simple," a golden opportunity awaits – an opportunity to not only reflect on your personal growth but to extend a hand of guidance to those yet to tread these pages.

A Journey Shared, A Compass Given

Imagine the thrill of discovering a treasure map that leads to buried gems of insight, answers to questions you've held close, and a pathway to smoother emotional waters. Yes, that feeling of unlocking hidden wisdom is second to none. Now, think of the joy you could bring to someone else's adventure by sharing your unique experience.

A Question to Ponder

Before we dive into the how's and why's, ponder this: What's more fulfilling than aiding a fellow traveler on their quest for growth? As you stand here, right in the middle of this book, you're in a prime position to make a lasting impact on someone's journey.

Unveiling the Power of Your Words

Leaving a review isn't just about showcasing your eloquence; it's about igniting a spark of transformation in others. It's about offering a guiding light to those who might be navigating the labyrinth of anxious attachment. Your review can be that reassuring signpost they need.

Becoming a Guidepost

Picture this scene: a curious soul, much like yours, scans the book's pages, seeking solace and enlightenment. Your review catches their eye – your words, your emotions, your experience. In that moment, you're not just a reader; you're a beacon of hope. Your review becomes a bridge connecting them to the very insights that shaped your journey.

Your Mission, Should You Choose to Accept

Now, let's get down to business. Your mission, should you choose to accept, is to venture to your preferred online bookstore and locate the space reserved for your thoughts – the review section. You're not just leaving a review; you're crafting a legacy, a legacy of empowerment and shared wisdom.

The Ripple Effect

As your words find their home amidst the digital pages, imagine the ripples they create. Your insights become a part of a much larger tapestry – a tapestry woven by fellow explorers like you. And remember, your review doesn't just stay within the confines of the book; it has the power to ripple through lives, inspiring growth and transformation.

A Hero's Reward

But here's the cherry on top: while you're extending a helping hand to others, you're also reaping the rewards. By joining this tribe of growth-seekers, you're connecting with a community that values positive change. Your words won't just be a gift to others; they'll be a testament to your commitment to growth.

Embrace the Call

So, dear fellow explorer, embrace the call. Take a moment to revel in your growth, then reach out and touch the lives of those who seek what you've found. **Head to this link if you read the e-book and pen your thoughts.** Your legacy of empowerment begins now, right in the heart of this book. Let's journey forward together, lighting up the path for ourselves and others.

Or scan the QR code below if you read the paperback version, then scroll down the page and find the option "Review this product."

Thank you for your participation in helping us and helping others!

Review this product
Share your thoughts with other customers

Write a customer review

5
Rewiring Your Brain for Security

Picture yourself back in the 1800s when America was bustling with activity. Phineas Gage was a regular guy, working hard as a railway construction foreman. People respected him for being responsible and calm. But guess what? Life had a big surprise waiting for him.

One spring day in 1848, things took a sad turn. Gage was doing his job, using explosive powder for construction work. Suddenly, a crazy thing happened – an iron rod shot through his head! Can you believe it? He survived, but things changed a lot after that.

Before the accident, Gage was like a rock – steady and reliable. But after the iron rod incident, his personality changed a lot. It was as if someone flipped a switch in his brain. He became impulsive and didn't act like himself anymore. He had trouble making decisions and keeping a job. The iron rod didn't just hurt his head; it messed with who he was.

As time went on, something amazing happened. Gage's story showed that our brains can change and adapt. Just like his brain restructured itself after the accident, our brains can change too. This ability is called "neuroplasticity." It means our brains can learn new things, adapt to different situations, and even heal from injuries.

Gage's story gave hope to others facing tough times. He showed that even when life throws you a curveball, your mind can heal and become strong again. It's like our brains are superheroes that can overcome challenges.

When we read about Gage, we see that his story connects with how we handle our relationships. Just like his brain changed after the accident, we can change how we connect with others. If we work on building better relationships, our brains can adapt just like his did.

Neuroplasticity isn't just a big word; it's something we can understand. Just like Gage's brain changed to cope with the accident, our brains can change too. We can learn new ways of relating to others and feeling more secure in our connections. Just like Gage rewired his brain after the accident, we can rewire our brains for better relationships.

Gage's story teaches us that our attachment style isn't set in stone. We can reshape our brain's pathways by thinking about how we relate to others. By understanding our feelings, challenging negative thoughts, and building strong connections, we're on a journey just like Gage's brain rewiring.

As Gage's story unfolds, we see how it's linked to the idea of neuroplasticity. He's like a guide showing us that we have the power to change our attachment style. His story is like a light, showing us the way to better relationships and understanding ourselves. In the big story of life, Gage's tale tells us that our brains are pretty amazing – they can rebuild, rewire, and help us overcome challenges.

What Is Neuroplasticity?

By reading about Gage's situation, we've already learned a few things about Neuroplasticity.

It's basically the brain's ability to form new neural connections throughout your life. Your brain is a wonderful structure that can adapt to experiences, learn new things, and recover from injuries. If you think about it, it's really the most important part of your autonomy.

Neuroplasticity helps us recover from brain damage or trauma, but it also comes into play when we learn new skills.

When someone's brain is damaged after a stroke and loses blood supply, other parts of the brain can take over some of the functions that were previously performed by the damaged part. Rehabilitation exercises can encourage the brain's neurons to keep on creating new connections. Sometimes it can even be a simple activity such as trying a new food or walking home on a different route.

Neuroplasticity can also come into play when you're learning new skills. For example, when you learn a new language, certain areas of your brain that are involved with language processing become more active. When you practice the new language, new neural connections form, and the language-related regions of your brain become more efficient. That's why it becomes easier to learn new languages with practice.

So, how does this work during the learning process? While we practice the skill we're learning, the connection between the neurons will become even more efficient, and the information will flow more smoothly. This is known as synaptic plasticity.

Hebbian plasticity occurs when we practice a skill, and the neurons involved fire together more frequently and strengthen their connections. This will help you perform the skill you've learned faster and more accurately.

You'll create new memories when you learn a new skill, which is closely tied to neuroplasticity. When you're sleeping and resting, the brain will consolidate these memories and further reinforce the neural connections related to the skill.

Learning motor skills, such as playing sports or riding a bike, also relies on neuroplasticity. With practice, the brain refines motor patterns, improving coordination and precision.

There are two main types of neuroplasticity, namely Functional plasticity and Structural plasticity.

Functional plasticity is your brain's ability to transfer functions from a damaged area of the brain to another area. This process plays an important role in rehabilitation. For example, if the area in the brain that deals with language is damaged, neighboring regions might take on language processing functions. This could also be the case for other bodily functions.

Structural plasticity is your brain's ability to physically change its structure in response to learning, experiences, and environmental stimuli. It creates new neural connections and changes the existing ones, which helps your brain work better.

Brain Rewiring: How Can You Boost This Process?

Maybe you've struggled with anxious attachment from a young age, which means you've probably always felt insecure and fearful in most of your relationships. You've experienced loss and rejection, which made it difficult for you to open up to others and trust them.

Neuroplasticity can help us overcome anxious attachment patterns by relearning our relationships. We can learn and develop new ways of relating to the people in our lives. When we experience secure and positive relationships, the brain will gradually change the neural pathways that are associated with anxious attachment.

For example, you could have core negative beliefs driving your anxious attachment style, such as believing that nobody will ever love you and that people will always leave you. You can challenge these thoughts and reframe them, to think about yourself and your relationship more positively. If you apply the process repeatedly, it will help your brain form new neural connections.

You'll feel more secure and confident in your relationships as your attachment style starts to change.

You deserve kindness and understanding, especially from yourself. Remember that while you might have children, and you could be responsible for other people as well, you won't be able to look after anyone else if you don't look after yourself first. If you're too hard on yourself and keep pushing when you shouldn't, it will lead to burnout in the long run. When you're kind to yourself, you can change your critical inner voice, which is the main driver for your negative thought patterns, which in turn contributes to your anxious attachment.

If you become more involved socially and manage to improve your support network, which makes you feel like you belong somewhere, it can also help rewire your attachment-related neural circuits.

If you're an introvert, you may find it daunting to have to go out there and start making friends. Don't worry. You don't have to push yourself or rush out there. It can be off-putting and stressful if you have unsuccessful social experiences. The reality is that there are unpleasant people out there who might not be interested in you or just be downright mean. If you should come across one of them, just remember, they're the problem, not you. They might be dealing with their own attachment or other emotional regulation issues.

You should consider gradually exposing yourself to social and other potentially challenging situations. This will help you grow and handle more challenging social experiences. If you do it this way, your brain will also be able to adapt and rewire over time. It will be more resilient and better able to handle stress as it goes through this process.

Seeing a therapist can contribute to your growth and learning experience if you don't feel like doing it on your own. Therapy is always a useful option, even if you just feel stuck in your life. A few sessions can help you see your life in a different light. A therapist can usually provide you with useful strategies and exercises you can use to help your brain rewire to be better able to deal with your anxious attachment style. This could include thinking about your early childhood experiences and trauma and how these could have shaped your attachment style.

Reading more about anxious attachment won't only help you understand better how to deal with this condition, but it's also a great way to stimulate your brain and encourage it to form new neural connections.

We've previously mentioned that keeping a journal will help you express your emotions and thoughts making your negative emotions feel less intense. The other benefit of this type of writing exercise is that it involves different types of your brain and can help you deal with your emotions.

Distractions and activities like learning a new language, or a musical instrument, can also help develop your cognitive abilities and promote brain plasticity. Exercise such as mindful walks can also help your brain rewire. This involves fully focusing on the environment around you as you walk by counting your steps, listening to sounds, and smelling the scents in the air. This is also a good way to reduce your stress levels.

Once your brain rewiring process is underway, you'll gradually start to feel more secure in your relationship, and you'll also need less reassurance from your partner and the other people in your life. You'll also become more confident once you're better able to manage your emotions.

In the next chapter, we consider how you can achieve secure attachment.

Activity: The Mindfulness Multitasking Challenge

The Mindful Multitasking Challenge encourages neuroplasticity by requiring that the brain should activate and adapt different neural networks at the same time. Taking part in different tasks can improve your attention span, cognitive flexibility, and task-switching abilities.

For this activity, you need a timer and a few simple activities. Make sure you're in a quiet space where you can't be interrupted.

You should use simple activities that use different senses:

- Fold the laundry while you listen to music.

- Chop vegetables while you recite a poem or the words of a song in your mind.

- Solve a puzzle while you focus on breathing deeply.

Set your timer for about 10 minutes, and then start with the task of your choice. While you're doing your task, pay attention to each action and the sensations you feel while completing them.

Pay attention to any distractions or frustrations you feel during the challenge. Then refocus on the tasks you have to complete.

After the timer goes off and you've completed your tasks, think about the experience. How did it feel to do many different tasks at the same time? Did you learn anything about your ability to focus and adapt? Write the answers in your journal.

Key Takeaways

- Neuroplasticity refers to your brain's ability to form new neural connections throughout your life.

- Your brain can adapt after experiencing certain things in your life and can also recover from injuries.

- When the brain is damaged, other undamaged parts can often take over the functions previously performed by the damaged parts.

- Learning new skills, such as learning a new language, can also encourage your brain to form new neural connections.

- Functional plasticity and Structural plasticity are the two main types of neuroplasticity.

- Neuroplasticity can also help you overcome anxious attachment patterns in relationships.

6
A Journey to Secure Attachment

In the world of relationships, I thought I had it all figured out. I considered myself someone with a secure attachment style – confident in love, open to communication, and pretty chill overall. But then I met someone with an avoidant attachment style, and suddenly, everything I thought I knew got thrown for a loop.

This whole thing started with a person who seemed to be a perfect match. It felt like fate brought us together, like we were meant to be. But there was this twist: she needed space. She wanted to take things slow, and I respected that. Then, out of the blue, two months later, she ended things. I was left feeling confused and searching for answers.

After that, I started questioning myself. Was I actually anxiously attached instead of securely attached? Looking back on the relationship,

I realized that she created a situation where I had to constantly prove myself. She made me feel like I had to work to keep her interested. She needed space all the time, and our connection was full of tests. It was like she needed to be in control.

I blamed myself for feeling anxious and unsure, but then it hit me. It wasn't me; it was her way of dealing with things. She projected her own doubts onto us, making me doubt myself. The more I thought about it, the more I saw that her attachment style was causing all the confusion.

Realizing this was a game-changer. I learned that it's important to trust your own feelings and not let someone else's insecurities mess with your head. Doubting yourself doesn't mean you're broken; it means you're growing. Getting support from therapy and self-help resources was a big help too.

For those dealing with anxious attachment, my advice is simple: don't let fear stop you from finding love. Embrace the present and don't let worries about the future hold you back. Just because you have avoidant tendencies doesn't mean you can't connect deeply with someone. It's all part of the journey.

Through this whole experience, I discovered that my secure attachment style was stronger than I thought. Even in the face of a challenging relationship, I didn't lose sight of who I was. This whole episode reminded me that attachment styles don't define us; they're just a piece of the puzzle. With each lesson learned, I got closer to understanding what it means to have a secure attachment – a path that not only changes how we relate to others but also rekindles the light within ourselves.

Do you feel trapped in a cycle of unstable and tumultuous relationships? Constant relationship ups and downs could leave you feeling exhausted. You might feel that you desperately want a more meaningful relationship that will bring you love and security, but you don't know where to start to get one.

Relationships can indeed be influenced by different attachment styles. Your fear of rejection or need for reassurance could have destroyed your past relationships. This might be an unpleasant realization to you, but it's a step in the right direction, as you've discovered the source of your problem. At first, you might worry that you will never be able to have a fulfilling relationship. However, you and your potential future partners deserve better.

You need to confront painful memories and emotions. This takes a level of self-awareness and means you'll have to do introspection. By putting in the work, you can gain a deeper understanding of yourself and recognize the patterns of anxious attachment that shaped your past relationships.

You'll find that your relationships will become more meaningful as you become self-confident about setting boundaries and communicating your needs. The fear that held you back for such a long time will be replaced with self-confidence.

This chapter aims to guide you from anxious to secure attachment. A willingness to grow and get the help you need can help you break free from the past and create a future of meaningful connections and relationships.

The upcoming book in this series will focus more on secure attachment, but in this chapter, we will provide you with some relevant information that can help you greatly.

What Is a Secure Attachment Style?

We all have family members or friends who exhibit secure attachment styles. They are often confident, friendly people who make life and relationships look easy. To those of us struggling, it may seem like they have a charmed life.

The main difference between people with secure attachment styles is that they interact with others in healthy and positive ways.

Maybe you have a happy couple like that in your friendship circle. You know, the ones who everyone says are soul mates in every way and who seem like they were made for each other. They trust each other and openly express their love for each other. They're also there for each other, even during life's ups and downs and through health and illness.

They seem to share a deep connection that you admire and also desire for your own life. While they're super close, they also don't spend all their time together. They each have their own group of friends, and every so often, they spend time apart and have weekends away with their friends. They do value their independence, and they also each have their own hobbies and interests.

Secure attachment is beneficial in so many ways. It's linked to lifelong mental health and better general overall well-being. You're less likely to experience anxiety and depression and have a more positive outlook on life in general.

You can take your first steps to develop a more secure attachment style by understanding the different attachment styles.

As explained earlier in this book, attachment styles are developed during childhood and will continue to affect your life into adulthood.

While your friends with secure attachment styles are able to communicate openly and honestly, you may struggle with trust and feel insecure in your relationships. You might also be an overthinker, which means that you'll want a lot of reassurance from your partner, which they will find emotionally draining.

When you're prone to overthinking, you can become trapped in a neverending cycle of rumination and overanalyzing your relationship, which in turn will lead to a cycle of anxious thoughts and worries.

What is rumination? This is a rather complicated technical term that is used to describe a simple, natural process. One way to think of it is that it's like a broken record in your brain that plays the same thoughts over and over. You may get stuck thinking about your relationship problems or something bad that happened in the past, and you just can't let go of these negative thoughts. You become anxious or sad, and before you know it, you're stuck in a loop of overthinking, which could even interfere with your daily life. You might be increasingly needy and unsure of your relationship, questioning every move your partner makes.

Securely attached people can deal with their emotions effectively, and they're pros at dealing with stressful situations and challenges. You'll find that they're confident in themselves and their relationships, and they don't feel afraid of losing people from their life if they come out and say what they think, even if they know their opinions aren't popular. They'll try to see the positives when a relationship ends. For example, maybe the person wasn't meant to be in their life in the first place, and there's someone better for them out there.

They rarely overreact emotionally and don't have mood swings and temper tantrums.

Step-By-Step Guide to Secure Attachment

Maybe this is going to sound a bit dramatic, but setting out to develop a secure attachment style can be described as setting out on an exciting journey to discover treasures within yourself. It's like an adventure, with its ups and downs, and some days you might even feel like giving up. However, keep on going because, in the end, it will be worth the effort.

There will be plenty of exciting developments along the way, and you shouldn't rush through them. Taking it slowly, and savoring every moment, will help you gradually build trust in yourself, strengthening your connections with others.

Embrace the challenges that will come your way during this journey, as this will help you find peace and comfort. Every step will make you more confident, as you gain more tools to build healthy relationships.

So, let's begin this amazing journey and go through all the steps. This is a rough guide, so you can do the steps in whatever way work for you. You could even add your own steps.

Step 1: Increase Your Self-Awareness

This may sound complicated, but it isn't. The best way to start is to think about your past relationships and look all the way back to your childhood years.

What were your experiences with your early caregivers? Write some notes on what you can remember. This could trigger your memory, and more important information could start to surface. Consider issues such as if you had mainly positive or negative experiences during childhood. Did you experience any trauma or abuse? How do you think these experiences have influenced your current attachment style?

Back to the present. Carefully observe your feelings, thoughts, and behaviors in your current adult relationships. Are you aware of any patterns of needing excessive reassurance, fears of abandonment, or out-of-control emotions? Do you tend to lash out at people in anger, or do you let others walk all over you while you try to please them?

Take note of these triggers that may cause anxious responses. Do you notice underlying emotions and beliefs that are causing these issues?

Step 2: Be Kind to Yourself

Once you've gathered all your important information, you can start working on yourself. Remember to be kind and patient with yourself as you undertake this important but challenging journey. It can be quite the building process to develop a secure attachment, and setbacks are part of the ongoing learning curve.

If negative thoughts and self-doubt threaten to overwhelm you, do your best to get them out of the way, but also, don't beat yourself up if you keep on having them. Everyone is vulnerable, and many people have gone through periods in their lives where they didn't like themselves very much. Looking for support is a sign of strength, and you should find help if you need it.

Step 3: Manage Your Emotions

You may have realized that you struggle to stay emotionally balanced, especially during stressful times. Maybe you argue with others, or you cope in unhealthy ways, for example, by eating too much unhealthy food. Don't feel bad about this, as all of us go through these periods in our life. It's all about how you learn to deal with it.

Mindfulness will help you stay grounded in the present and will make it easier to notice your emotions without judging them.

It will also help you if you can recognize and identify your emotions accurately. For example, "anger" and "sadness."

Deep breathing can also help you calm down during difficult times.

Step 4: Listen and Express Yourself

Express your feelings and needs as openly to your partner as you can. It depends on how much emotional expression both of you are comfortable with, but you should feel comfortable sharing your vulnerabilities, as it encourages emotional intimacy with your partner.

You also need to be open to listening to your partner and understanding their perspectives. Treat them with empathy and kindness. For example, if they're having problems at work, try to understand how they feel about it, and don't blame them for anything.

Sometimes, they may want you just to listen so that they can unburden themselves, and they won't expect you to say anything. People can feel calmer and more emotionally in control by simply unburdening themselves.

Step 5: Build Trust

Building trust in a relationship can be easier than it sounds, but you need time and patience. The main thing is that you need to be consistent and reliable. Turn up when you say you will, and don't make excuses when you mess up. For example, when you forget date night or you work late without letting your partner know, you'd have a good excuse.

However, there also needs to be patience and kindness between partners. Forgiveness is also important if your partner makes a mistake. Nobody is perfect, and we're all going to get it wrong some of the time and make our partner angry with us.

It's also important to be authentic with your partner. They want to know the real you, and you can only really build a stable long-term relationship with someone if you know each other's authentic selves.

Step 6: Set Healthy Boundaries

You need to be clear about your personal boundaries and values, and it's essential that you communicate them respectfully to the people in your life, including your partner. For example, your partner might enjoy going out and regularly wants to attend social events, while you might enjoy spending more time at home. In this case, you would need to come to a compromise where you agree to attend a certain number of social events in a month, or perhaps that you won't stay too late and would go home at a time that was reasonable to you. You need to make sure that at least some of your partner's needs are met while not neglecting your own.

Setting boundaries could also refer to something such as how much of the housework each of you would be accountable for. There can often be frustration in relationships if one partner finds they're solely responsible for running the household and looking after children while having to work full time as well to be able to contribute to the household budget.

Also, remember to respect your partner's boundaries and recognize their autonomy. Your partner may need alone time or some time away to hangout with friends. Respect that this might be an important part of their identity.

Step 7: Guidance and Support

Once you've tried all the previous steps, and you may feel that you still need more guidance, it might be worth your while to see a therapist.

Support groups or workshops focused on attachment and relationships can also help you on your way to gaining secure attachment. The advantage of joining a workshop is also that you can connect to others who are on the same journey as you. Sometimes, sharing thoughts, ideas, and anecdotes with people who are in a similar situation can give you a new perspective and help you feel more comfortable with your journey. It can be a confidence booster if you learn you're going in the right direction. If you're dealing with some difficulties, input from other people might help you see where you can make changes.

Step 8: Practice and Patience

Finally, it's all about practice. Change takes time, and you're going to have to be patient with yourself. Relationships involve ongoing work and commitment. Even when you've managed to reach a state of secure attachment, you won't be able to sit back and just let your relationship run independently. A relationship is like a job, you constantly need to be putting work into it.

In the next chapter, we look at how you can build trust in your relationships.

Question Sheet: Building Secure Attachment

This worksheet is designed to help you build secure attachments in your relationships. Take your time and reflect on each question honestly. Write your answers in your journal.

Understand Your Attachment Style

Think about your past relationships and early experiences with caregivers.

Identify any patterns of attachment that you notice secure, anxious, avoidant, or disorganized.

Recognizing Emotional Needs

List three emotional needs that are important to you in a relationship, e.g., trust, affection, and support.

Open Communication

How do you communicate your feelings and needs to your partner or loved ones?

Do you think you can improve your communication style?

Setting Boundaries

Identify three personal boundaries that promote your emotional well-being.

Are you comfortable expressing these boundaries to others? If not, why?

Emotional Regulation

Think about a recent situation where you experienced strong emotions. How did you handle them?

How can you manage your negative emotions in a healthy way?

Building Trust and Forgiveness

How did past conflict affect your trust in a relationship?

Could you rebuild the trust?

Quality Time and Affection

Write down a few activities or gestures that make you feel loved and appreciated.

How often do you engage in these activities or receive these gestures?

Supporting Each Other

How do you support your partner or loved ones in pursuing their dreams and goals?

How would you like them to support you?

Reflecting on Growth

Describe one area in your relationship where you have seen growth and improvement.

How did you contribute to this positive change?

Key Takeaways

- If you have a secure attachment style, you interact with others in a healthy, positive way.

- People with secure attachment styles have confidence in their relationships. They're emotionally secure and comfortable when it comes to expressing their emotions.

- Securely attached people express their feelings openly and in healthy ways.

- You can improve your attachment style throughout your life. You can start your journey by working on improving your self-awareness.

- Open and respectful communication is the glue that holds healthy relationships together.

7

Building Trust in Relationships

Dear Husband,

As I sit down to write this letter, I find myself looking back at the past twelve years of our marriage, I see the ups and downs that shaped our story. It's like a roller coaster of feelings and moments that brought us to where we are today.

When we started, everything felt like a fairytale. Love, marriage, kids – it was like a dream come true. But as time passed, we got lost in the craziness of life. I became the mom who took care of everything, while you worked hard to provide for us. We both had our roles, but somehow, we drifted apart.

I gave my all to our kids and our home. But somewhere in all that, I lost a piece of myself. I felt guilty whenever I thought about taking time *for me. You were there, but sometimes, it felt like you were far away. I wished you could see how much I needed your help, even though I never said it out loud.*

As the years went by, something changed between us. We stopped being just us and became "mom" and "dad." I didn't know how to tell you that I needed more from you. The hurt and frustration built up inside me, and I wished you could understand without me having to spell it out.

Then came a moment that shook our world. An emotional affair that I got caught up in. It didn't go far, but it was a wake-up call. Our marriage was in trouble, and we needed to fix it.

Counseling became our lifeline. At first, I was angry at you for not being there for me. But as we talked and shared, something changed. I saw my own mistakes, my own walls that I had built. I realized that I was avoiding problems instead of facing them.

It hurt to admit it, but I had been carrying around my own baggage. My past made me think I had to be perfect to be loved. And I expected you to know my needs without me saying a word. But that wasn't fair to either of us.

Through tears and tough conversations, we started rebuilding. It wasn't easy, but it was worth it. I opened up about my mistakes, and you listened. You let me see your side too, how you struggled with conflicts and misunderstandings.

Step by step, we rebuilt trust. We let each other in again, sharing our fears and hopes. It was scary, but it was also a relief. I learned that I could be imperfect and still be loved, and you learned that being there meant more than just paying bills.

Now, we're on the other side of that darkness, holding each other's hands. Our story isn't the same as before, but it's better. We talk more, we understand each other better, and our love is stronger.

Today, as I write this letter to you, I want to express my gratitude for our journey. It wasn't easy, and there were moments when the road felt impossible to tread. But we did it. We faced our demons, rebuilt the trust that was eroded, and emerged on the other side with a renewed sense of purpose.

This letter isn't just a reflection of our journey; it's a testament to the strength of our love. We've proven that even in the darkest of times, there's a flicker of light that can guide us forward. Let's continue this journey, hand in hand, and keep rediscovering the "us" that's always been there, waiting to shine.

With all my love,
Your Wife!

When it comes to relationships, you want to make sure you've surrounded yourself with nurturing and supportive people. The kind of people you have in your life will affect not only your mental but also your physical health.

While it's always nice to have some excitement, you also don't want to deal with people constantly causing conflict and drama. If you are in a relationship with someone like this, it might be difficult to trust them. You may still expect someone to behave or react in a certain way, and if they overreact to something you say or something that happened, it would be difficult to trust them again. For example, if you have an anxious attachment style, you may find yourself clashing with those who have an avoidant style. Someone who values their independence might get stressed out by a partner who needs constant reassurance. It could be that you want your partner to respond to your messages or calls almost immediately, or at least soon, while they see nothing wrong with not responding when they're busy at work. You might feel like you're being ignored, and this causes your stress levels to rise. This could also cause you to stop trusting them, as you might tell yourself that they're having an affair and that they're planning to leave you.

If you're already in a relationship, you could always work on your attachment style, and your partner could do the same. It's important that you're able to overcome small qualms together, especially if you want your relationship to continue well into the future. If you're only stepping out on the dating scene now, ideally, you should try to find a partner with a secure attachment style, although this isn't always black and white

You should look for people who make you feel like you're being understood and appreciated. You should feel relaxed around them and that you can trust them to treat them in certain ways. If you feel like you have to walk on eggshells around someone, it's probably not healthy to have them in your life.

When you've been in a relationship for a while, you might feel that your bond is not as strong as it once was. It might even feel like you and your partner are like cars on the freeway, always rushing past each other in opposite directions. It's easy to drift apart, especially if you've been married for a few years and you have children and jobs that keep you busy. Often, when you finally have time for each other, you feel too drained to connect.

The danger in not asking each other for what you need is that you can start to resent one another. Your partner might not even be aware of your unhappiness and continues to think that they're pleasing you and that you have a successful relationship. Unspoken needs can only lead to problems in the long term, such as burnout and a breach of trust, which can't easily be repaired.

Marriage counseling can help you address your underlying issues, but you will also need to put in the work. You need to realize when your expectations are unrealistic and where you may need to change them. Open communication and forgiving past mistakes can help you renew your relationship. Consistent effort can help restore most relationships in the long run and help you create a loving relationship in which both of you feel cherished.

Building Trust Between the Different Attachment Styles

In every relationship, trust is the foundation on which you build your behavior and interactions. It's the glue that keeps your special bond together. If you trust someone, they make you feel safe and secure, and you don't have to worry that you'll be judged when you share your thoughts and feelings with them.

Trust can make your connections more meaningful. Without trust, your relationship will be shaky, like a house without a base. It's a red flag if you feel on edge with your significant other. If you find yourself in a toxic relationship, it's in your best interest to get out as soon as possible, but that's a whole other topic for a different book.

If you have an anxious attachment style, you could struggle to trust even your partner, as your fear of rejection is so strong. The fear of abandonment can overwhelm relationships if you didn't have trustworthy relationships as a child. You may need constant reassurance from your partner that your relationship isn't about to end. It's easy to misinterpret minor, unimportant cues as signs that your relationship is in trouble. For example, if your partner is feeling unwell and they don't want to talk to you, it doesn't mean they're tired of you and want to end the relationship. Once they've recovered and their energy levels increase, you'll be number one on their to-do list again.

Jealousy and possessiveness will only strangle your relationship with your partner and create more tension. You could even struggle with trusting most people in your life, not only your romantic partners. If you have a deep-rooted mistrust of others, it will only damage your relationships. When you keep people at a distance, it will be difficult for you to form deep and meaningful connections with others.

Building trust in a relationship can be hard work, and it can also take a long time. In a sense, building trust starts with really listening to each other. You need to understand each other's perspectives and needs. When your partner is speaking to you, give them all your attention. Don't try to think of how you're going to answer them while they're still speaking. It's always best to get the relevant information before considering your reply. You can only really understand their perspectives and needs if you listen to them attentively. This will also make your partner feel safe when they speak to you, and they'll be much more likely to share.

You also need to know that you'll respect each other's boundaries, as this is also an important aspect of building trust. If your partner needs some alone time to recharge, you should respect that and not be too demanding until you see they're ready to be approached.

Being consistent and reliable in your words and actions builds trust over time. Keep your promises and commitments to show your partner that they can rely on you. For example, if you promise to help with household chores, make sure you do this every day and not only once in a while when you expect to give something in return. If you've promised to take your partner on a date, be on time, and honor your commitment to them. Don't cancel, especially not without letting them know, as this will make a serious dent in the trust in your relationship.

If you've messed up in some way and hurt their feelings, apologize sincerely, and do something to make up for it. Acknowledge the impact of your actions and express your remorse. You and your partner should forgive each other for mistakes and then work together to move forward. Holding onto a grudge will only make it so much harder to rebuild trust.

This may seem obvious, but sometimes we still fall into the trap of committing these offenses, which could cause irreversible damage to our relationships. Lying about something significant, or cheating on your partner, can push your relationship beyond the point of no return. If you betray your partner, it could shatter their trust, and it could take a long time to rebuild it, even if it's still possible.

Our partners may sometimes unexpectedly react in ways that we don't understand or that make us angry. That is why we need to be aware of what might have triggered this behavior.

We need to be able to discuss our triggers openly and sensitively, as this also creates a safe space for us to understand and support each other. For example, you may want to discuss future plans with your partner, who is triggered by commitment discussions since their previous partner ended their relationship very suddenly and unexpectedly. While you're enthusiastically chatting away, you notice they're becoming distant, and they even react defensively to some of the questions you ask them.

You might be frustrated, but do your best not to push them away, and instead ask about their feelings and also tell them what you've noticed. If you treat them with empathy, they will hopefully feel safe to open up about their past experiences. You should also give them time to deal with their emotions, and when you get together for a similar discussion, first talk about how you can talk about certain things in ways that are comfortable to both of you. You need to keep potential triggers for both of you in mind.

If you know your partner is going through a difficult time, you should also show them support and help them understand that you're there for them during both the good and bad times. Try to understand when they have a difficult boss or work projects that have failed, and they need to put in overtime and extra hours at work. Or, they could have a sick family member, and they need to spend hours visiting them at the hospital or at home. As soon as they're able, they'll make up for the time they lost with you. It will only do damage to your relationship if you place additional stress on them at a time when they're already down and just trying to keep their head above the water.

Why Are People From Different Attachment Styles Attracted to Each Other?

It might seem strange that people with completely different attachment styles would be attracted to each other, but it happens. There are some good reasons for this, and sometimes it just happens when people meet and are instantly attracted to each other. We all know that feeling when we meet someone and just feel there's something special about them. Only later, when the first exciting phase of the relationship is over, we then realize that our attachment style is completely different from that of our exciting new partner.

You've probably heard the saying, "opposites attract." You might even have wondered why you're attracted to people who are very different from yourself, even though you think they're not actually a great match for you. Once you're involved with them, you just can't get enough of them.

You could be drawn to someone with a completely different attachment style because you feel they offer you something unique. You've been with others who are more like you before, and you just quickly become bored of them. While you want closeness and reassurance, anxious attachment, your partner values independence and space, avoidant attachment. It's a challenge, and like puzzle pieces, you need to fit together.

You and your partner's different emotional needs and communication styles can make your interactions passionate and exciting. It can also be compared to mixing different colors to create a unique work of art. Your relationship is so much brighter than one that had been drawn with one colored pencil.

So, as you can see, we could often find ourselves attracted to people who have an attachment style that clashes with our own, for example, a couple where one partner has an anxious attachment style while the other one has an avoidant attachment style, or one of the partners could even have a secure attachment style. Relationships like these may have their ups and downs, but if you and your partner work together, you can make it work.

So, which attachment styles go together well?

Two securely attached people will experience less stress in their relationship, as they've learned from their primary caregiver during childhood how to care for another person. They're usually also better at regulating their emotions. Many stable, long-term relationships have at least one securely attached partner, as they'll be able to care for the other partner who might have attachment issues.

An insecure, anxiously attached partner could also adapt and develop a more secure attachment style if they learn and feel comfortable. Often they're able to learn a better attachment style from their securely attached partner.

Is it possible for attachment styles just not to be compatible? Once you're past the first exciting part of your new relationship, you'll come to see more of how your partner deals with conflict and if they're emotionally available. We often don't notice these things at first when we just start learning about each other, and we're so excited about going out together and discovering new places with our partner. There may be seeming incompatibilities, but the different attachment styles can also learn to be compatible.

One of the most important things is to learn to deal with conflict. Partners who may have different insecure attachment styles will have to take care of how they act during conflict and disagreements if they want their relationship to last.Shouting and screaming at each other never has a good outcome, especially if you call each other nasty names that you can't take back later. Remember that words can hurt just as much as causing someone physical pain.

People with different attachment styles are also often attracted to each other, as the attraction might be based on some wound they received from a caretaker during childhood. We often choose our partners based on the early experiences we've had with childhood caregivers, even if their attachment styles are very different from ours, as partners who remind us of people from the past feel familiar. They make us feel comfortable in a way, even when they're not good for us. You'll often end up staying in a toxic environment because this is what you have been used to experiencing. It's also possible that you're hoping to receive the love you didn't get from your parent from a similar type of person when you're an adult.

It might not be that easy to recognize at first that your new partner's attachment style is very different from your own. However, you shouldn't become despondent because it's possible to learn more about your partner's style and to grow in the relationship. While being with someone from a different attachment style can be challenging, it can also be a great learning opportunity and a chance to develop your self-awareness. You might find yourself confronting insecurities and discovering new things about yourself. It could even be an adventure, and you'll learn exciting things about yourself that you didn't think were possible. The right partner can add meaning to your life and even get you to do things you were scared of trying before.

Making Your Relationship Work With an Opposite Attachment Style Partner

Sometimes, it may feel impossible to make a relationship work with someone who has a completely different attachment style from your own.

You're holding on to your partner for dear life and want to be as close as possible to them while they're using all their energy to pull away because they say you're suffocating them. They say they need recovery time and can't spend all the hours of the day with you, while you're perfectly happy to do just that.

First, you need to investigate and figure out how you ended up with a partner so different from yourself.

If you see yourself as too clingy and "too much" in a relationship, you're likely going to subconsciously end up in relationships that make you feel like that.

You will keep attracting someone who makes you feel and think in this way about yourself. That's why anxious and avoidantly attached people keep attracting each other, as a relationship between them allows them to keep thinking these things about each other.

The anxiously attached person will tell their avoidantly attached partner that they're emotionally unavailable, while the avoidant tells their anxious partner that they're too needy. So they send each other the messages that one is not enough and the other is too much in their relationship.

So, once you realize your partner has an opposite attachment style, is there a way to make it work?

When you're in a relationship like this, you need to learn as much about your partner and their needs and behavior as you can. Try to discover what really makes them tick without judging them.

You need to keep an open mind in relationships like these and not look for reasons why your partner isn't meeting your needs. The relationship will only be heading one way if you're only interested in proving that your partner isn't great. It's also up to you to keep a positive mindset when things go wrong.

You need to be considerate of your partner's needs and treat them with kindness. If you've dated enough people with this attachment style, you'll know what your partner's emotional needs are and how they're going to behave. Try to use the knowledge of mistakes you've made in the past to your advantage in your current relationship.

It's about give and take and being considerate towards each other. You'll need to give your avoidant partner some space, while your avoidant partner needs to give you some attention. If you're the more talkative or people-oriented person in the relationship, encourage your partner to have an open discussion about these issues.

Allow your partner to be in their attachment style, and don't expect them to change their entire state of being for you. One attachment style isn't better than the other one, even if the secure attachment style is regarded as the ideal. You can grow together, though, and both of you can make changes to your way of interacting and being.

Modern Technology and Your Attachment System

We all use modern technology, such as cell phones and other digital devices, to communicate in our relationships. This often makes communication less direct and could also cause misunderstandings between people, especially if you have different attachment styles. Someone with an avoidant attachment style could use this form of communication to avoid discussing certain topics with their partner, while the anxiously attached might become stressed when they don't receive immediate responses to their messages. If you're anxiously attached, and you desperately need that reply, it's unfortunately also too easy to bombard someone with text messages with the hope that you will receive a reply sooner.

For example, let's look at a text message conversation between one partner with an anxious attachment style and another one with an avoidant attachment style. Lucy has an anxious attachment style, and she wants constant reassurance from Alex, who has an avoidant style and is starting to feel overwhelmed by her need for constant attention and reassurance. While he wants to be independent at times and feels he needs space to recharge, his behavior then makes Lucy feel more anxious and insecure about their relationship. She will often need more attention from him, which has made him think about ending the relationship.

Example: Text Messages Between Partners With Different Attachment Styles

Lucy: Hey, Alex. I just wanted to say I miss you so much! I can't stop thinking about you, and I hope you're thinking about me too. Are you busy at work?

Alex: Hey, I've been thinking about you too, but I'm busy at work right now. Can we catch up later?

Lucy: Of course! But I just need to hear that you still love me. I sometimes worry that you find me boring and that you'll lose interest in me.

It takes several minutes for Alex to respond with the following message. In the meantime, Lucy becomes increasingly anxious.

Alex: Can we talk about this later? You know I care about you, but it gets a bit overwhelming when I constantly have to reassure you. I really have to focus on work now.

Lucy: I understand. I'm just afraid of losing you. Sorry if I'm being too much.

Several minutes pass again, and Lucy is getting scared that this time he's not going to respond when her phone buzzes.

Alex: It's okay, Lucy. I'm in a meeting at the moment. Can we talk about this when I'm not at work?

Lucy: Okay, I'll try to give you space. What are you doing tonight?

Lucy starts to feel anxious when Alex doesn't respond after an hour. She begins to think that he possibly really doesn't want to see her anymore. She decides to contact Alex again after several hours have passed.

Lucy: Alex? Babe?

Alex: I still have to do a lot of work tonight. Maybe we can meet up over the weekend?

Alex is tired after a difficult day at work, and even though he wants to spend time with Lucy, he just doesn't have the energy to deal with her today.

Lucy is disappointed, and her stomach is in knots. She had hoped that he would spend time with her sooner.

Lucy: Okay, how about going to see a movie on Friday?

There's no response from him until he finally replies at 7 p.m. She is anxious, but she tells herself he is busy at work. Lucy tries to reassure herself, but she can't help but worry about the situation.

Alex: I will probably still have to catch up on work on Friday, but how about we get together on Saturday?

Alex is actually free on Friday, but he is starting to feel smothered by Lucy and would rather use the time to relax and recover before seeing her the next day.

Alex and Lucy's relationship is an example of how different attachment styles can cause friction in a relationship, especially where electronic communication is concerned. Anxiously attached people want immediate responses, while others are often busy and just can't respond to them immediately.

If you have a partner with an avoidant style or someone who is very independent, they may become overwhelmed by your constant need for attention and not respond to you immediately.

If you want your relationship to last for the long term, you'll have to discuss your different styles and work at understanding each other.

In the next chapter, we're going to take a look at how you can stop sabotaging yourself in relationships.

Activity: Trust Evaluation Worksheet

This worksheet can help you and your partner figure out if you need to work on trust issues in your relationship. Answer the questions independently, and afterward, discuss them with your partner.

Factors Affecting Trust

List the factors that have positively or negatively affected your trust in the relationship.

_____
_____
_____

Communication

Do you and your partner discuss your trust issues openly?

Are you comfortable doing this?

_____
_____
_____

Past Trauma

Have you experienced trauma, and how is this affecting your ability to trust?

_____
_____
_____

Honesty

Do you feel your partner is being honest in your relationship? Are they open to discussing their actions and emotions?

_____
_____
_____

Consistent Actions

Does your partner consistently follow through on promises and commitments?

_____
_____
_____

Handling Conflict

How do you and your partner handle conflicts about trust issues?
Do you manage these conflicts in a healthy and constructive manner?

_____
_____
_____

Support and Empathy

Is your partner supportive when you express trust-related concerns?

_____
_____

Do you believe your partner understands your feelings and fears about trust?

_____
_____
_____

Personal Boundaries

Do you and your partner respect each other's boundaries and privacy?

_____
_____
_____

How do you feel when your partner sets boundaries? Does your partner react in a negative way when you set boundaries?

Trust-Building Efforts

What efforts have you and your partner made to build trust in your relationship?

_____

_____

Do you think you and your partner need to do further trust-building?

_____

_____

Future Trust Goals

What are your individual and shared goals for building and maintaining trust in the relationship?

_____

_____

How do you see yourself having a trusting relationship with your partner in the future?

_____

_____

Reflections

Take the time to think about your responses. Have you learned anything valuable from this evaluation?

_____
_____
_____

Key Takeaways

- Trust is the foundation that holds relationships together.

- Relationships become shaky when there is no trust.

- People with an anxious attachment style often struggle with trust due to experiences of childhood neglect, abandonment, or abuse..

- These people may want constant validation from their partners.

- Anxiously attached people tend to overanalyze their partner's actions, words, and behavior. They have a tendency to misinterpret minor cues as signs of rejection. They could also be dependent on their partners to an almost suffocating extent.

- Building or rebuilding trust in a relationship can be a long process that needs commitment from everyone involved.

- You need to be able to communicate with your partner openly and honestly to build trust.

8
Overcoming Self-Sabotage

Unfortunately, individuals with an anxious attachment style may sometimes face challenges in finding happiness. Your anxious mindset could also have originated in childhood if you experience neglectful or abusive relationships with your caregivers. Remember, it's never your fault; you deserve happiness. Anxiety can cause your self-sabotage, as you may think you don't deserve to be happy, this isn't always a conscious way of thinking, and you could even think that a terrible disaster will befall you if you're actually happy.

Self-sabotage is very unfortunate, as it will destroy your success and happiness and lead to missed opportunities and lost relationships, which can take a terrible toll on your life.

When you're anxiously attached, you doubt and fear the affection of your loved ones, and you have a tendency to push people away from you. Your fears and insecurities can seriously get in the way of you forming bonds and meaningful relationships with others. This might be a depressing thought, but it's possible to end this cycle of self-sabotage by doing introspection and becoming more aware of who you really are. To be able to have healthy relationships with others, you really have to know yourself inside out.

Stop Self-Sabotaging Behavior

When you're aware of the destructive things you're doing in your life and what damage it's causing you, you can make a conscious decision to break free from them.

If you know what type of self-sabotaging behavior your attachment style is causing, you can work on making an end to your sabotaging tendencies.

Self-sabotaging behavior can, unfortunately, create a negative feedback loop in your relationship. Your need for frequent reassurance can cause your partner to get overwhelmed and pull away from you emotionally. This can make you feel even more anxious, and the cycle of self-sabotage will continue if you don't make an intentional effort to stop it.

If you struggle with communicating openly and you overthink and catastrophize, it could also cause you to self-sabotage.

If you internalize your worries and you don't share them with your partner, you could become increasingly frustrated and resentful. This will also create distance from your partner if they're unaware of your feelings and struggles. Unresolved conflicts can simmer and escalate over time until some kind of explosion occurs that harms your relationship.

Beware, especially, of catastrophizing, as this means you'll just focus on the negative parts of your relationship. A minor problem might suddenly seem like the end of the world. This type of thinking will only make you doubt yourself more, and your partner may disconnect from you when they get too overwhelmed and emotionally drained by this type of behavior. If you're always dwelling on the negatives, it will just create discontent in your relationship. If your mindset is always negative, you'll also put your partner in a bad mood.

The other danger is that through your constant worry and fear, you may create a self-fulfilling prophecy for your relationship. You could unknowingly change your behavior to fit your negative view of things and become more defensive, clingy, or distant. This type of behavior will just create tension and conflict in your relationship.

The unintentional behaviors and reactions stemming from self-fulfilling prophecies can cause your communication to break down with your partner. Misunderstandings and conflicts will just perpetuate the cycle of self-sabotage.

You can also sabotage your relationship by not being emotionally intimate with your partner. If you don't share your true thoughts, feelings, and fears with your partner, your relationship can't grow. It will stagnate and stay superficial, and there will be no deep connection.

If you hide your true feelings, your partner may not understand your behavior or emotions, and this could cause misunderstandings in the relationship, which could cause you to become even more emotionally distant from each other.

By not sharing your true feelings, you may also be denying yourself the emotional support you need from your partner.

There are ways to stop sabotaging yourself. Take notice of your thoughts, and ask yourself if negative thoughts are affecting your behavior and what you could do to improve the situation. You should realize that many of them are likely not even true, and you should try to replace them with more realistic views of yourself. For example, if you think your partner is working late because he doesn't want to spend time with you and he finds you boring, think about the exciting and fun times that you spent together before. Think about all the things that make you a fun and interesting person to be around. If you think you're lacking in certain ways, e.g., your partners know more about certain things than you do, you could always do courses to learn more, and this could even lead to you finding a new career and becoming qualified and successful in an entirely new field that you haven't even thought of before. What a great way to achieve personal growth! In general, we become more secure and successful in our relationships if we're also more confident in ourselves. If we know and embrace our own strengths, we're less likely to sabotage ourselves.

If you find that you're unintentionally sabotaging yourself in many different areas of your life, you need to create an action plan and set meaningful goals for yourself. You need to consider what creates meaning and purpose in your life and what energizes you.

Don't let your emotions control you or determine the outcome of your relationships. It's important to learn to manage your emotions by taking part in activities like yoga, meditation, deep breathing, and Mindfulness. Mindfulness keeps you grounded in the present and helps separate your thoughts from reality. It can help you deal with problematic situations and people.

Building Self-Confidence and Worth

Building your self-confidence and self-worth can help you reduce self-sabotage in relationships. If you feel positive and secure in yourself, you'll be less likely to become involved in self-destructive behavior that can harm your relationships.

Self-confidence is about believing in yourself and your abilities.

Imagine you're learning to ride a bike for the first time. If you have self-confidence, you'll trust that you can balance and pedal without falling. Even if you wobble a little at first, you believe you'll get better with practice. Similarly, you might struggle when you're learning to drive, but if you're confident that you'll improve, you'll get better with time, especially if you practice regularly.

Having self-confidence means you feel capable of tackling challenges and trying out new things. You have a positive inner voice that tells you that you can do things and that you shouldn't doubt yourself.

So, how do you build confidence if you struggle with anxious attachment?

Building self-confidence can be difficult if you struggle with the deep-rooted fears and insecurities that are associated with this attachment style.

If you tend to overthink and catastrophize minor issues, you can become stuck in a cycle of worry and self-criticism, which can get in the way of your attempts to build self-esteem. One of the tricks to deal with this is to focus on your thoughts and try to deal with negative thoughts as early as possible. You should try to distract yourself, even if it's only for a short time, to top yourself from ruminating about unpleasant issues.

Relying on other people for validation can also stop you from developing authentic self-assurance, as your self-worth depends on other people's approval. You'll have to address your fears, challenge your negative thoughts and accept yourself as a human being that makes mistakes like anyone else. Life's not about being perfect but about learning from and not repeating your errors. Becoming a dedicated lifelong learner and accepting yourself as a wonderful work in progress is important.

Working on your assertiveness is also important for building your self-confidence, as it will help you express yourself authentically. If you practice your assertiveness, you're proactively shaping your relationships and your future well-being.

Activity: Self-Sabotage Awareness

This worksheet will help you become more aware of your self-sabotaging behaviors. Complete the following exercises in your journal.

Reflection on Self-Sabotaging Behaviors

Think about past situations where you may have engaged in self-sabotaging behaviors. These could be moments in relationships, careers, personal goals, or any other aspect of your life. Write down a brief description of each situation.

Developing Coping Strategies

Think about healthy coping strategies that you can use when you feel the urge to engage in self-sabotaging behaviors. These strategies could include deep breathing, seeking support from a trusted friend, or engaging in a favorite activity to relieve stress.

Creating an Action Plan

Based on your reflections, patterns, and coping strategies, create an action plan for stopping self-sabotage. Set specific and achievable goals to implement your coping strategies when faced with triggers.

In the next step, we'll reflect on our journey so far, and consider the next steps we need to take.

Key Takeaways

- Many of us sabotage our own success and happiness.

- This could cause us to miss opportunities and lose relationships.

- People with anxious attachment styles have a tendency to self-sabotage.

- Anxiously attached people can also sabotage themselves by overanalyzing situations, catastrophizing small issues, and imagining worst-case scenarios.

- This can also cause your partner to feel emotionally disconnected and jeopardize your relationship.

- Negative outcomes that are the result of self-fulfilling prophecies can validate the negative assumptions you have about yourself.

- Anxiously attached people can also hinder the development of emotional intimacy in their relationships by not being vulnerable to their partners.

- You need to find the root causes of your self-sabotaging behavior, and you can do this by enhancing your self-awareness.

- You can also stop sabotaging yourself by setting meaningful goals and starting to work on an action plan.

- You're less likely to sabotage yourself if you replace your inner critic with a friendly voice.

- Building your self-confidence and self-worth can also help you reduce self-sabotage.

- Having self-confidence means you feel capable of tackling challenges.

9
Reflection and Next Steps

The only way that we can live is if we grow. The only way that we can grow is if we change. The only way that we can change is if we learn. The only way we can learn is if we are exposed. And the only way that we can become exposed is if we throw ourselves out into the open. –C. JoyBell C.

This powerful quote reminds us of the connection between change, growth, learning, and vulnerability. These words are very relevant as you start your journey to developing a secure attachment.

Growth is an essential part of life. Just as a flower must grow towards the light to bloom, we, too, must grow to be able to lead meaningful lives. We can only achieve growth if we're willing to change and challenge our existing beliefs and behavior. Continuously learning and growing is such a rich and valuable experience that will not only add meaning to your life but also to the lives of everyone you hold dear.

Remember that you're never too old to learn. Even if you only start your journey later in life, you can still change your existence in fantastic ways.

We can only achieve change through learning as we try to understand ourselves and our attachment styles better. However, as the quote reminds us, learning comes with exposure. To heal and develop secure attachments, we must be willing to be vulnerable and open ourselves to the truth of our emotions and experiences. We need to heal old wounds to be able to create genuine connections with others.

Growth and healing are not linear processes. You could take two steps forward and then another three steps back, but as you continue learning, you'll make up for the time you lost. It takes courage and patience to navigate the complexities of attachment styles, but with each step of self-discovery and self-compassion, you move closer to a more secure and fulfilling way of relating to yourself and others.

Continued Growth and Lifelong Learning

Continued growth and lifelong learning are vital aspects of leading a meaningful life. Personal growth can be a slow marathon, but every small step taken to improve yourself can be significant in shaping your character, moving away from an anxious attachment style, and enriching your relationships and life experience.

Life is always changing, and continued growth and learning enable us to adapt to new circumstances, challenges, and opportunities. It equips us with the skills and knowledge to deal with life's challenges with resilience and flexibility.

Lifelong learning involves exploring new ideas, experiences, and perspectives throughout your life. This journey of self-discovery fosters greater self-awareness, which allows us to understand our emotions and beliefs. Not only can it help us in our personal lives, but it can make us more successful in our careers, especially during these challenging economic times, where the phrase "unretirement" is becoming ever more popular, as people have to work for longer, or they continue working for themselves for the remainder of their lives. This ongoing journey of self-improvement can add purpose and fulfillment to your life.

Learning will broaden your horizons. It will expose you to diverse cultures, perspectives, and new knowledge and will help you become more empathetic and open-minded.

The continuous support of knowledge also encourages innovation and creativity. Learning from different disciplines and experiences can also help us approach problems from different angles and find innovative solutions.

You're more likely to thrive in our rapidly changing world if you embrace continuous growth and learning. Lifelong learners are more adaptable and open to change, making them better able to benefit from new opportunities.

The influence of continued learning and growth also goes much further than our individual lives. We contribute to the collective growth of society when we share our knowledge and skills with others.

Activity: A Self-Reflection Exercise

Self-reflection is the most important thing you can do if you want to work on your attachment style. We need to understand why we react in certain ways before we can change anything about the way we do things.

Find a quiet space where you can sit and focus. Make sure that you have your journal with you, and write down answers to the questions below. You can also make notes on any of your electronic devices if you don't want to use pen and paper.

Ground yourself first in the present by doing a mindfulness exercise. Recognize the feelings you're having at the time, and think about why you're having them.

Consider what the core values are in your life, and write them down. Why do you think these things are important to you?

What emotional needs do you have when being in a relationship? Are you able to express them to your partner?

How has your attachment style impacted your behavior and relationships? Has its influence been negative or positive?

Name three qualities that contribute to your growth and connections with others.

Write down positive affirmations that you can use to challenge your negative thoughts.

Consider areas in your life where you need to grow and improve. Set goals for yourself to improve in these areas. Remember to regularly check on the progress you're making in achieving these goals.

Visualize your authentic self, and write down some notes on who you expect this person to be. Are you already living as your authentic self, or do you still need to do a lot of work to get there?

Key Takeaways

Growth is an essential part of life, and we need to continue growing to add meaning to our lives.

We need to heal wounds from the past to be able to form better connections with others.

Personal growth can be a slow but meaningful process.

Lifelong learning will help you become more empathetic and open-minded.

You're more likely to thrive in the rapidly changing modern world if you embrace continuous growth and learning.

Conclusion

We hope you've enjoyed this marathon and that you've built and strengthened your relationship muscles along the way. Now that I've helped you unlock the secrets to building secure and fulfilling relationships, you can say goodbye to your anxious attachment patterns.

A new life, filled with love and success, is within your reach. You've already started undergoing positive changes when you started reading this book, and now you just need to keep on going in the right direction. After all, life is all about growth, positive change, and making your existence more meaningful.

Key Takeaways

We believe the knowledge you gained from the book will be invaluable and stay with you for a long time. Remember that you can always read the book again or even just reread certain chapters to refresh your memory.

The book focuses on the following key takeaways:

We've shown you why you react the way you do in your relationships. The mystery of your attachment style has been unraveled, and you now know more about how it affects your self-esteem and love life.

You would have learned some strategies and coping mechanisms to help you cultivate secure attachments and build healthy relationships.

The aim of the book is also to help you boost your self-esteem and to help you be kind to yourself, which lays the foundation for making your life more fantastic than it already is.

As interesting and inspiring as our attachment journey has been, we also need to be real. Personal growth takes time and work, and you can't just change your life overnight. However, we encourage you to love and appreciate yourself as a work in progress. Strive to be better, but also enjoy and appreciate your life where you are in it at the present time. Remember, it's all about progress and the journey, not the destination and achieving ultimate perfection.

We've got one little request before we part ways. Your support means the world to us, and we would be grateful if you would share them with us by leaving a review on Amazon. As we stated previously at the end of Chapter 4 your feedback is invaluable to us as writers and to those who find themselves in the same shoes you were in before delving into this book.

Scan the QR code below for paperback and share your thoughts (if you haven't yet), or click here if you read the E-book.

Then scroll down the page and find the "Review this product" option. You got this!

Thank you so much for taking part and helping this book be extra special and for making a big impact on many people.

We also encourage you to look out for the next book in this series, which will be coming soon. You've taken the first steps to create better relationships with this book, so continue the journey and strengthen your skills with the next installment.

We look forward to embarking on another journey of discovery with you.

Until next time.

S.C. Rowse & Inner Growth Press

References links

Use this link or scan the QR Code provided.

They'll take you to a Google Drive file where you'll find all the resources we used to make this book.

It's like a treasure trove of information that helped us create what you've just read. So, take a look and enjoy exploring these useful materials!

When Feeling Deeply Meets Understanding Deeply

Imagine a world where emotions hold a special key to connections, where some people can sense feelings as if they were their own. This chapter explores the surprising ways in which anxiously attached individuals and empaths, those who feel others' emotions strongly, share a unique bond.

What's an Empath?

An empath is someone who feels other people's emotions deeply. It's like having a radar for feelings, where they can tell what others are experiencing, even without words. It's like being a sponge that soaks up emotions. Now, let's see how this relates to those who are anxiously attached.

Feeling Others' Feelings

Anxiously attached people are really good at understanding the emotions of the people they're close to. They can tell if someone's happy, sad, or worried, often before anyone says a word. But when they step into the world of empaths, something interesting happens.

Connecting Through Emotions

In the realm of empaths, both anxiously attached folks and empaths find a connection. They both put a lot of importance on feelings and understanding them. For anxiously attached individuals, this means they can connect with people more deeply, like two puzzle pieces fitting together. They understand the power of emotions, just like empaths do.

Sharing Feelings, Sharing Strength

Both groups also share something special: vulnerability. Anxiously attached individuals might worry about being left alone, while empaths might feel overwhelmed by others' emotions. But this vulnerability isn't a weakness—it's a source of strength. It's like they have a secret code to understand each other's struggles and fears.

Speaking the Same Emotional Language

Anxiously attached, people step into the empath's world and discover a new way to communicate—through emotions. It's like having a secret language that needs no words. This language helps them connect on a level that's beyond what's said out loud.

Exploring Further and Connecting Deeper

As we wrap up this chapter, we've only scratched the surface of the fascinating world where anxiously attached individuals and empaths meet. If you're intrigued by the power of emotions and the unique connections they create, there's so much more to discover.

To delve deeper into the realm of empaths and uncover the intricate threads that bind us through feelings, follow the link below. You'll find a treasure trove of knowledge waiting for you, ready to take you on a journey of understanding and self-discovery.

So, here is our invitation for you to explore our other books as well.

Each one offers a new perspective, a fresh insight, and a chance to expand your horizons. Whether you're curious about emotions, relationships, or the mysteries of the mind, there's something waiting just for you.

So, why wait? Embark on this journey of discovery, connection, and learning. The world of empaths is calling, and our collection of books is here to guide you every step of the way. Click the link, or scan the QR code, dive in, and let the exploration begin!

Printed in Great Britain
by Amazon